THE HOLY TRINITY

Dumitru Stăniloae

The Holy Trinity

In the Beginning There Was Love

Translated by Roland Clark

Foreword by His Beatitude Teoctist
Patriarch of the Romanian Orthodox Church

HOLY CROSS ORTHODOX PRESS
Brookline, Massachusetts

Published by Holy Cross Orthodox Press
50 Goddard Avenue
Brookline, Massachusetts 02445

ISBN 978-1-935317-31-9

Originally published in Romanian as *Sfânta Treime sau la început a fost iubirea*, Editura Institutului Biblic şi de Misiune al Bisericii Ortodoxe Române, Bucharest, 1993; reprint, 2005.

On the cover: Fresco from the Church of St. Basil the Great in Zvorăneşti, Neamţ, Romania. © 2010 Vasile Grosu.

Library of Congress Cataloging-in-Publication Data

Staniloae, Dumitru.
[Sfânta Treime sau la început a fost iubirea. English]
The Holy Trinity : in the beginning there was love / Dumitru Staniloae ; translated by Roland Clark.
p. cm.
Includes bibliographical references (p.).
ISBN 978-1-935317-31-9 -- ISBN 1-935317-31-8
1. Orthodox Eastern Church--Doctrines. 2. Trinity. I. Title.
BX323.S72513 2012
231'.044--dc23

2012005095

CONTENTS

Foreword

The dogma of the Holy Trinity has always been at the center of Orthodox theology, which is why it was an endless subject of reflection for Fr. Dumitru Stăniloae, may he rest in peace. The special place that the Trinity occupies in his teaching on the Church makes Fr. Stăniloae the theologian *par excellence* of the Holy Trinity in the contemporary world. In fact, his entire corpus is a mammoth effort to place the unspeakable mystery of the Holy Trinity at the center of all recent Christian life and thought. As with St. Maximus the Confessor, whose work he has translated and commentated on in Romanian, this dogma does not represent an isolated theme for Fr. Stăniloae. His exegeses of the Trinity glimmer throughout every chapter of his dogmatic theology. While identifying both a united absolute essence and distinct absolute hypostases at the heart of the Holy Trinity, in the most Orthodox spirit Fr. Stăniloae always aimed to bring the living, dynamic personalism of Orthodox Christian theology into the light.

Speaking as no one else in contemporary theology has about the infinite value of the person, about its unfathomable depths, and seeing "the undying face of God" in man, Fr. Stăniloae can also speak about the perfect love whose only source is the Holy Trinity. He tellingly calls the Trinity the supreme structure of love: "God is love, and therefore light and life in themselves, because He is the supreme unity of three individual Persons in communion with one another" (p. 14). Thus it should come as no surprise that the title of this work is *The Holy Trinity: In the Beginning There Was Love*. The love between the Persons of the Holy Trinity preceded creation and was the motive force behind the *ex nihilo* creation of the world and of man. This love embraced the whole design so as to make it, through the deification of humanity through grace, a partaker of the untold goodness of God. But as Fr. Stăniloae says, "In order to reach this state and unite themselves with supreme existence . . . created beings need to make an effort of their own free will" (p. 7). Using this liberty without wisdom and responsibility, however, is always the bringer of suffering, decadence, and death—beginning with our forefathers' fall into sin. It means giving in to the egoism of the passions, suffering the spiritual blindness that results, and leaving the communion that gives life to holy love.

Humans receive from the Holy Trinity the ability to remain in this communion because one of the Triune Persons—the Son—took our human flesh upon Himself, sacrificing Himself for fallen man and raising him to the fullness of the divine life in communion with the Father and the Holy Spirit. As Fr. Stăniloae shows, man was created and then saved by the Triune God with an eternal process of deification in mind, an unending growth in love. For this reason, it is no accident that the book ends with several beautiful and moving prayers to the Holy Spirit, through whom "the entire dialogue between God and human beings takes place" (p. 87). The Holy Spirit teaches us that man can carry on this dialogue with his Creator and Savior only through a purposeful and responsible existential engagement, which confirms the truth that love and self-sacrifice are inseparable.

Blessing the new edition of this precious book, we desire that those who seek sustenance and spiritual light in these pages will come to understand, not only with the mind but also with the heart, that at the basis of this world, of all visible existence—

which appears increasingly shaken, tried, and divided—stands the eternal love of our unshakable, perfect, omnipotent, and only Savior: the Holy Trinity.

His Beatitude Teoctist (+2007)
Archbishop of Bucharest,
Metropolitan of Wallachia and Dobrogea,
Locum Tenens of Caesarea in Cappadocia,
and Patriarch of the Romanian Orthodox Church

PREFACE

The Holy Trinity is the supreme mystery of existence. It explains everything, and nothing can be explained without it. This is why it is intelligible even though it is a mystery, and also why it is logical up to a point. The Holy Trinity is presented as a real metaphysic, as the abyssal but somehow intelligible foundation of all existence. Philosophers who speak about metaphysics lack any clarity with regard to it. For them, metaphysical reality is nothing but an essence ruled by an evolutionary law or a series of emanations from which everything else flows. Their theories reveal that reality is dependent on something, but they cannot explain what it is. The metaphysics of the philosophers thus shows itself to be without logic.

At least in terms of our reasons for trying to understand the Holy Trinity—in terms of the sense that it gives to existence—it satisfies the requirements of logic. It is love without beginning, and seeks love's expansion. What can justify existence more than love? Love can be endless because it is never satiated by anything. Having no end, it can also have no beginning. Love without beginning or end sheds light on and brings a complete thankfulness for existence. The metaphysics of the philosophers, which is blindly subordinated to an uncreated and unending law, gives no light.

The second thing that I want to mention in this preface is that the Orthodox Church sees the Holy Trinity as the love of God that works through the Holy Spirit in the souls of believers, in order to raise them into the loving relationship between its Persons. For this reason, the sacraments have a decisive importance in believers' lives. In them the Holy Trinity works through the Holy Spirit in their souls. In Catholicism the sacraments provide nothing but a created grace through which merit is accorded to believers as a result of the suprameritorious sacrifice of Christ. Other forms of Christianity that have broken away from Catholicism no longer have any space for the mysteries (the sacraments) in their lives. Orthodoxy has an accentuated spiritual and sanctifying quality. The sins of Orthodox believers are not forgiven only in a legal sense, as they are for Catholics in this life and for Protestants in the next, but the power of Christ is communicated to them, through His Holy Spirit, so that they may love God and their fellow humans. Together with love, believers find freedom from selfish passions and a holiness that increases in accordance with the efforts that they themselves put in.

Orthodoxy does not only know a Christ of words but one who, loving the Father through the Holy Spirit, communicates the love of the Holy Trinity to believers. Orthodoxy helps believers grow in holiness through ascetic practices so that they might sanctify themselves through the power of the Trinity, in which they live even while on earth, growing in the kingdom of love without end.

Fr. Dumitru Stăniloae

Chapter 1

The Meaning of Existence

We cannot imagine that once there was a time when there was nothing. St. Gregory of Nazianzus says this in many places. At one time he says, "All 'is-ness' (God is saying [in Exodus 3:14]) is mine, without beginning or ending."[1] Where did existence come from if it was not from eternity? Existence without beginning, or from eternity, is an inexplicable mystery. Yet at the same time the mystery explains everything. The existence that we know is a causal one, but how could things with a cause and a beginning exist if there were no existence without beginning or cause?

It is therefore possible to say that we know about uncaused and unknown existence—or divinity—from things that are caused and known, and we understand existence that is unknown from that which is caused. There is a reciprocal communication between cataphatic and apophatic knowledge, the apophatic being partially known through the cataphatic, and the cataphatic being better understood through the apophatic. The apophatic is not entirely unknown, just as the cataphatic is not completely understood because it originates in absolute apophaticism.

We know caused things from their laws, from their state of dependency. But their laws, or dependence, presuppose an uncaused existence that is independent and "absolute." Uncausability and independence have an "absolute" quality that remains a great mystery for us. Nonetheless, the fact that existence not only contradicts caused and dependent things but actually explains them makes it possible for us to have some knowledge of them. Even so, this knowledge leaves a greater part of its object unknown because our understanding is accustomed to using laws to explain caused and dependent things, which are made subject to those laws by another existence over which those laws have no power.

Apophaticism is not complete unknowing, and cataphaticism is not total knowledge. We discover something about the ultimate cause of creation thanks to known things, yet we do not even understand these things completely because we never fully know their ultimate, uncaused cause. Apophaticism throws light on cataphaticism, but it throws a mystery as well. Cataphaticism does the same: we know neither cataphaticism nor apophaticism completely, and through them we discover the mystery. Thus we can use what we know from the caused world to learn something about its cause, the greater part of which will still remain unknown.

A negative knowledge of caused things teaches us that any existence that is uncaused, eternal, or of itself must be of a spiritual order, because the spiritual—even in the reduced form that we live it—is to a large extent free and not subject to laws. But existence that is independent and without beginning or end, which is complete in itself, could never be entirely in and of itself if there were some law in it that explained it. In this case, it would not be complete in itself, totally independent, but would depend on a law that it had to think about, or that helped it to think and to explain itself. Such a being would no longer be total existence, for the law on which it would depend would have to be thought of separately from existence itself. And how could a law be thought without a being to think it? Such a law would have to be imposed by another being. There must be a being somewhere that has no superior law, but which is a law in itself by virtue of being supreme—a being that is both law and liberty from the very beginning.

It is not possible to affirm that there existed without beginning from eternity a being that was constrained by a law that said that it eventually had to produce self-consciousness and liberty. On the one hand, this hypothetical being must necessarily produce consciousness, and on the other hand, it is free to choose what it will do. Liberty cannot be the product of a necessary law applied without choice.

On the other hand, if that law subsequently appeared in a being that had no beginning, this would mean that prior to the law's appearance it was necessary for it to emerge, and that some time had to pass before it did. But how could time appear in a being that had no beginning, which is to say, in an eternal being? How could a time arise in this being as the condition of an evolution leading to the appearance of self-consciousness? It is inconceivable how, in eternity, a "moment" could occur through which time and evolution could begin. Would this not mean that eternity always had a temporal character? But can we imagine eternity with a temporal character? Is not this formula a contradiction in itself? Does it not mean, on the one hand, an existence without beginning, and on the other, time, which includes a beginning, an evolution, and an end point at which it reached consciousness? And does this not mean a certain limitation, an inability in this being that therefore cannot be in and of itself and without beginning? Moreover, is it not logical for us to think of a being that exists through itself from eternity, not subject to any laws and not needing to become subject to any? Furthermore, does it not make sense for us then to think of it as having a consciousness that is not dependent on any laws that would be external to or greater than itself? Is it not absurd to conclude that in this being that exists through itself there appeared a moment in which a law emerged in a necessary manner—a law that had existed virtually in it before, from eternity—so that on the basis of this law the being would arrive at a consciousness of itself or at an explanation for its existence? Could a law subsequently appear in an eternal being, and then self-consciousness on the basis of this law? Is it not absurd to admit that a law and self-consciousness appeared at a given moment in an eternal being without its volition? Would this not mean reducing that being that existed through itself to a being that is not through itself but that is an addition to a law that already existed virtually in it? And how far could we go in our search for the origins of this law?

In fact, it is impossible to define "being" as an existence that has its beginning in itself. But one thing must be acknowledged: it cannot be without self-consciousness in and of itself, through a law that is subject to it. It is thus an existence of a completely spiritual order, not needing anything additional to explain it. Moreover, if a being that exists of itself from eternity can appear, then such a being can have no end. Evolutionary laws that lead toward an end cannot appear so long as no such law gave it a beginning.

We find laws in ourselves and in the world that we are tied to, then we use these laws to explain ourselves as humans. But where could these laws have come from—where could our own self-consciousness have come from—if there were no eternal being that was not subject to laws but that was capable of giving laws to inferior being? This being would need to be superior to and the first cause of these laws, which themselves evolve toward an end.

So many beings that are subordinated to laws have self-consciousness, but where could that self-consciousness have come from if there were no superior being to give laws in the first place? And where did their thirst for self-consciousness come from? This self-consciousness is linked to an ever-greater knowledge of everything. It is significant that these dependent, conscious beings do not only aspire to a deeper knowledge of themselves but also to a direct relationship with absolute existence, with existence that is of itself, in which everything is subsumed and explained. Man is not satisfied with living in his own relativity and with other relative beings. He wants a relationship with the absolute so as to gain the possibility of living in the unlimited and endless absolute. Man is a being who knows that he is not complete in himself, and so he cannot be without a beginning, because all that could possibly exist is not contained within human beings. But at the very least, man must have his own self-consciousness.

What would he be without self-consciousness? If man does not even know where he came from or that which he is a part of, what more can he expect? There must be a being in itself, perfect from eternity, in which there is nothing that preceded it.

Descartes produced the formula "*Cogito ergo sum.*" He thereby tightly bound thought, or awareness, to existence. Being is the condition of thought. But the connection is stronger than that. Thinking is not simply *a* form—it is *the* most certain form of being. Consciousness is the most definite form of existence. It is self-determined existence. If existence is in itself a light, consciousness is a light turned toward oneself. "*Cogito ergo sum*" does not mean "thought," but thinking is the most certain sign of my existence. There are other forms of existence that do not manifest themselves in thought, such as rocks, grass, plants, irrational animals. But they exist in order to give content to man's thinking and consciousness. My first thought is of my own existence, which is to say that my existence is thinking itself. But my consciousness is strengthened by the consciousness of others, and then by the unconscious being of other things in the world that exist for this very purpose.

Eternal being, which held all forms of existence virtually in itself, and only in itself, could think of everything and be conscious of all. It thereby assures the existence of everything. I have knowledge, and thus consciousness, of that which I am mostly thanks to my progress in knowledge through relationships with things that are different from me. Socrates could say "I know that I know nothing" because he only knew existence partially. He knew himself, but he knew that what he knew about others was incomplete. Does not this thirst for knowledge, manifested in Socrates' somber judgment, show that somewhere there exists a perfect knowledge that encompasses all existence? Does it not show that man is created to move toward a knowledge of everything and that therefore, somewhere, there exists a consciousness that knows all and that does not have to climb toward a higher goal?

There was a light that had no beginning, which could bring all created lights into being through the words "Let there be light!" All of creation received existence in order to enhance the light, or the consciousness, of man. At its base, everything that "is," is light. There could not be an "is" from eternity that was dark, which moved toward an "is" that was illuminated by an evolving consciousness. From this comes the conclusion that time did not appear out of eternity in existence by itself. It had to be made. There had to appear a temporal being that was different from that which existed from eternity; created by it, not emanating from it. And this being could be nothing but the creation of an existence that was of itself from eternity, for time could not produce itself through itself, nor could it be an emanation of an existence that was through itself from eternity. It had to have another cause.

There are two planes of existence: one eternal, existence of itself; and one temporal, created by that eternal being that has the power to create the second plane from nothing, and not as its natural offspring. If there were only the divine form of existence, it would lack omnipotence and generosity. If there were only the worldly or pantheistic form, subordinated to laws that do not freely bring happiness to another form of existence, that would again represent an incomplete form of existence.

To return briefly to the unity between the cataphatic and the apophatic, we should add that it can be expressed as the unity between the rational and the mystery. The rational contains the mystery in itself, and vice versa, both in God and in the created world. But the connection is different for both. In the created world the rational leads us to the mystery, to the mystery of a creation that is not of itself but that presupposes a being that is of itself from eternity. It leads us, that is, to the mystery of God as the rational explanation of the mystery of creation. And our reason implies, as does its explanation (which is its mystery), God as its supreme Reason.

According to St. Maximus the Confessor, the intelligences of this world reveal the mystery of God to us. There is no contradiction between the mystery of God and the reason of the world. Our reason is created in order to know that reason that has at its base the reason of God the Word: "The rationality of things, given by God according to His wisdom before time began . . . is seen by understanding things. For all the things of God, which we contemplate in our flesh, with the help of the appropriate science and knowledge, tell us in a hidden way about how they were made. Through them we learn of God's purposes in every created thing. . . . Through the wise contemplation of creation, we discern the Reason which sheds light on the Holy Trinity, which is to say, on the Father, the Son and the Holy Spirit."[2]

In the end, all existence, beginning with the eternal and unseen God and ending with the world created for life in God, is both rational and mysterious. All being is a mystery that humans cannot explain. But everything is also rational, having the goodness of God and happiness in Him, as its fount and goal. There can be no total emptiness, nor any being without a purpose.

In summary, we can say that there is a metaphysic that is identical with the supreme Spirit and that explains the created world in which we live as a phenomenal world, dependent on that Spirit, not evolving out of it but created by it from nothing. Yet this phenomenological order itself exists to be raised from its state of being subordinated to laws of development. Conscious things must follow such laws in order to rise up toward an ever-closer unity with existence of itself. That existence experiences goodness and love in itself as an identity between the highest expression and the fullest joy of living in liberty. Even the body, formed from matter and especially subordinated to laws, will be raised above those laws through resurrection, being spiritualized, or deified; and the entire universe together with it.

Because it is without beginning, supreme existence is eternally happy in and of itself without needing to develop at all. In order to reach this state and unite themselves with supreme existence, created beings need to make an effort of their own free will. They can only progress through that freedom that has been given to them as they follow laws that are an expression of the good will of God, or of supreme Reason. But once reason has been given to them, they can use it to oppose the good that supreme Reason and its laws demand of conscious things. They can use reason in a distorted manner to justify orienting themselves toward deceitful goals, or to promote their own egoism. Goodness desires to rest in a free harmony established among conscious things and between them and God. But selfishness opposes the good, and therefore opposes God. It ruptures the Reason that brings harmony among all things, and between everything and God. This shows once again that creation too must contribute something if it is to have unity with God. But the Holy Trinity, in which the most perfect harmony and love reside, helps creation make its contribution. The Son of God Himself helps humanity realize this unity. The Father uses the Son, just as He uses Reason, for the sake of creation.

It can be said that the Triune God is also the God of true Reason, understood as the force of goodness and harmony. Again it is St. Maximus the Confessor who develops this idea. A monopersonal god would not give himself as the model and power behind harmony. He would not have anyone equal with himself who could draw near to humans, fulfilling the role of mediator between God and men, and among men themselves. St. Maximus the Confessor presents the preincarnate Son of God as the Reason according to which everything was created, and the incarnate Christ as the one who once again brings harmony to creation, and between creation and God. This is because true Reason is one with love; and a monopersonal god would not have love as the power to create the world and as the purpose of creation. The world is created by the incarnate Son of God to receive Him into it. For all love comes from Him, in all the stages through which men have to pass during their lifetimes, so that in Him all may love the Father and thus love each other.

> Christ Jesus, the Word of God, as the Maker [Creator] of all, also made the natural law [i.e., the law of natural harmony]. And as the Cause and Giver of laws He gave, certainly, both the law written in letters and the law of the Spirit, which is to say, the law of grace [of the gospel]. For "the end of the law," which is to say, the written law, understood spiritually, "is Christ" [Rom 10:4]. So if in Christ as Maker [Creator], as Cause and Giver of laws,

> and as Redeemer, the natural law, the written law, and the law of grace are brought together, this adds truth to the words of the holy Apostle that God will judge the secrets of men according to His gospel [cf. Rom 2:16], which is to say that He judges according to the good news that He brings.[3]

Noting the reciprocity between the mystery of God and the rationality of creation, or seeing mystery and reason in both, we could leave the impression that in the godly Reason, which is in part apophatic, there is really no mystery that surpasses either the rational or the mysterious sides of creation by too great a margin. In fact, the divine Reason is "higher than reason," as St. Maximus the Confessor says. It has an infinitely deeper apophatic content than the rational content that is visible in creation. In God the apophatic surpasses the rational to the extent to which His being surpasses created reason. Neither of them is easy to understand. St. Gregory of Nazianzus says, "I penetrated the cloud, became enclosed in it, detached from matter and material things and concentrated, so far as might be, in myself. But when I directed my gaze I scarcely saw the averted figure of God [Exod 33:22–23]. . . . Peering in I saw not the nature prime, inviolate, self-apprehended (by 'self' I mean the Trinity), the nature as it abides within the first veil and is hidden by the Cherubim, but as it reaches us at its furthest remove from God."[4] St. Gregory of Nazianzus calls the "averted figure of God" that he saw "the 'majesty' [of the divine nature] inherent in the created things he has brought forth and governs."[5] Unlike Plato, who says that God is "difficult to know but impossible to describe," St. Gregory says that "to tell of God is not possible . . . but to know him is even less possible."[6]

But "not only does God's peace pass all thought and understanding . . . but so does exact knowledge of the creation as well. You can be sure that we possess but the bare outline of the creation. . . . Yes, far more than these things does their transcendent cause, the incomprehensible and boundless nature pass understanding. I mean understanding what that nature is, not understanding that it exists. Our preaching is not vain, our faith empty [1 Cor 15:14]. . . . Conviction, you see, of a thing's existence is quite different from knowledge of *what* it is."[7]

We do not perfectly understand the rationality behind creation either, in which "the averted figure of God" is reflected. Creation too is somewhat apophatic. But the being of God, whose "averted figure" is seen in creation, is far less known. From this point of view, Socrates was right to say "I know that I know nothing," if we translate this as "I know that I know nothing exactly," and for that reason I cannot claim to know anything as it truly is. But given our meagerness, what we know of the immeasurable greatness of God is nonetheless enormous. It is extremely important that we know *that* He is, even if we do not know *what* He is.

Is it not something of infinite importance to know that there exists one who is uncaused, higher than all that is caused, and who explains the existence of all knowledge, people, and love? Does it not throw a gigantic light upon everything to know that there exists one who is infinitely higher than everything in the world, and who is from this point of view indescribable and apophatic? Does it not cause me to understand that all the good that I experience and all my eternal, meaningful hope is from Him, as is the salvation that comes to me in Christ? This is not enough to save me, but, happily, it gives sense to my life. And is not this knowledge, on the other hand, helpful for cultivating my knowledge of Him? How wonderful it is to know that being who is beyond my understanding, who gives us everything without us giving anything!

Do I know the full mystery of my fellow human being, who loves me and does good to me? And yet, how much happiness does it bring me to know him at all? It is a knowledge that encompasses both the humility through which I know his unfathomable depths and my gratefulness for everything that he gives me. The more I see him as unfathomable, the more good it does me. I see that I am more pretentious when I think of myself as his equal or better. And the less I understand his existence, the less he expects me to serve him, while he serves me all the more.

Chapter 2

Thirsty for Infinity

I showed in the last chapter that self-caused existence, or existence without a beginning, must have a full consciousness of itself and of everything that is contained within it both actually and virtually. This self-caused existence has no need of anything, and has everything in itself. This means, as the Church Fathers say, that it is life itself. Through their thirst for it, created things show that they also desire such a life or being. Humans too experience this desire as necessary, but it is not unlimited in them. Unlimited plenitude of experiencing this life must exist somewhere, for otherwise why would humans thirst for it? And the desire for such a life, or such being, gives the possibility of and motivates self-caused existence to want to extend itself in their lives. This is why we are created with a thirst for it and capable of sharing in it. And how could our thirst for infinity be explained if infinity did not really exist somewhere? In a sense, even matter gives humans the power to live well through bodies once they are controlled in a holy manner.

God wants life, or the good that He is naturally and infinitely, to extend into limited beings through His help. A general pantheistic existence, in which everything happens according to certain laws, cannot be seen as something that promotes goodness. The pantheism of the philosophers, which argues that all existence exists and moves according to laws that impose themselves in some inexplicable manner, explains neither the unquenchable thirst for the good nor its possibility.

Existence through itself, as fullness of life or of being, encompasses everything that now is and everything that can have life from eternity. It can be seen in the following three forms: (1) The first is goodness or the loving will to give. And this shows that there is not only one Person, but two or three eternal Persons, who give and are given to fully. We also see in full existence the will to give to people created from nothing, so that they may have the joy of existing in unity with such an existence and among themselves. (2) But it also places omnipotence in the service of this unlimited goodness, which desires that limited created things enjoy its love, with a joy that gives them the power to love and to draw nearer to infinite goodness. This omnipotence of the eternal Persons, which is placed in the service of goodness, is further seen in the fact that limited things do not fear liberty because they want to freely enjoy the love of the eternal Persons. Yet if they do not use their liberty in this way, they do not cease to exist, which again shows the unlimited goodness of the eternal Persons. (3) The fullness of existence through itself is also shown in the consciousness of everything that is, for there is power in consciousness as well. And the knowledge of the other two cannot be missing from this consciousness.

Goodness, united with God's knowledge and omnipotence, flows endlessly through the created world. God does not hesitate for a moment to use His omnipotence and omniscience to benefit all that which His goodness has created. Even the worst trials, which come to some because they do not make use of His goodness, can be useful to others. But God's uncaused existence willfully puts His goodness into action. If the exercise of His goodness were not voluntary, it would no longer be goodness. And the fact that this free movement of goodness could not be but from one person to another shows that the supreme being is an interpersonal being. This means that nothing that happens in created existence can be considered to be the sole product of an extending automatism. Even though automatism also has a significant role, it was begun and is sustained through the personal will of God as an aid for conscious creatures in their free efforts toward growth in goodness.

God is above the laws, and the automatism that they partly sustain. He moves with a liberty that, although it also sustains this automatism, often creates deviations from it through miracles, which are given to spiritual beings so that they might know the good He has in store for them. *Man does neither good nor evil through compulsion, automatically,* although he cannot do all the good or all the evil that he chooses. This helps us understand that God is complete freedom, but His freedom, accompanied by unlimited power, is the exclusive source of the good. Humans can nonetheless choose not to accept all the good that God offers them and guides them toward.

The Christian conception of existence differs from pantheistic, emanationist, or evolutionist conceptions. In the Christian worldview, the freedom of both angels and humans plays important roles alongside the actions of a good and free God. Even with their freedom, however, angels and humans cannot reduce the material or spiritual realms in which they were placed to total disorder. I mentioned that the pantheism of the philosophers, which believes that all existence moves only through laws to which it is subordinated, laws whose origin cannot be explained, cannot account for the appearance of the good. For it, the good purely and simply does not exist.

I mentioned three principle elements of God's being: unlimited goodness, omnipotence, and a complete knowledge of everything. But there is a unity among these elements. Goodness, or love, is the most solid form of life; omnipotence is that which produced the unique existence of God and which allows it to progress, or, if it does not progress, does not let it lose everything; and knowledge is also placed in service of the good. God's being (that is, His good and happy life), power, and knowledge cannot be weakened or limited. These elements cannot be weakened except in existence created from nothing, in which they are gifts that can be accepted or refused. When they are received, they grow through the efforts that created beings themselves make. When they are not accepted, creation itself becomes deformed. Power is placed in the service of egoism, and egoism falsely assumes that it can grow infinitely in life and knowledge, using arguments and dishonest judgments in an attempt to strengthen itself.

This undermines the communion between people, because the self comes to be thought of as the supreme goal of existence. Goodness or love that is focused only on the self is no longer goodness or love; power is replaced by weakness, and knowledge is limited to a false privileging of the self, which is identified with everything, leading to great darkness. There is no longer room for drawing near to God as a loving Trinity of Persons.

The Apostle John emphasized with extraordinary clarity the relationship between goodness/love and knowledge/light, which is life. This connection applies to humans too. He says, "He who loves his brother abides in the light . . . but he who hates his brother is in darkness and walks in darkness, and does not know where he is going, because the darkness has blinded his eyes" (1 John 2:10–11).[1] God is love, and therefore light and life in themselves, because He is the supreme unity of three individual Persons in communion with one another. Estrangement from God brought darkness, as love and power were lost.

All the forms of God's essence have in themselves the power to communicate. But because God is not obliged to communicate them, they communicate themselves, within Him. This means that God is in three Persons who communicate being (or life), goodness, and light (or knowledge) among Themselves. This makes God a Trinity of Persons united in the greatest possible love. A lack of communication produces evil and ignorance, because the fullness of life, goodness, and knowledge is also lacking. Such a state belongs only to the created world, which does not have life, goodness, and knowledge as part of its essence.

The three forms of God's essence, of existence that is of itself, can be considered to be truth in all its plenitude. Thus Jesus Christ called Himself God incarnate and the truth. He said of Himself, "I am the truth and the life" (cf. John 14:6). And if knowledge discovers the truth and so is one with light, Christ could say of Himself, as of the one who is the truth, "I am the light of the world." And if light is knowledge of the truth, He could say about Himself that "he who walks in Me does not walk in darkness." So He identifies Himself also with love.

Thus, in the following words of Jesus, through which He says that He is the light, we must see also the affirmation that He is love. He even says directly that this light is life: "I am the light of the world. He who follows Me shall not walk in darkness, but have the light of life" (John 8:12). The Apostle Paul also says this about Christ when he calls Him "the power of God and the wisdom of God" (1 Cor 1:24). As power He is also life; and as wisdom He is light and love. All these form the content of the essence of God, and in Him they are unlimited. Having everything in Himself, He is the fount from which these things come to us. As the Son of the Father and having these things together with the Father, Jesus Christ is of the same essence as the Father.

Because they do not have these things through themselves, the essence of created things is neither unlimited nor does it exist of itself. But even though they do not have it through themselves, they have it through the creative act of God. This implies not only that they are limited and dependent on God, but also that they are necessarily linked with God's essence in all its forms. Thus they have the capacity to receive this content in a limited manner, and even thirst to have it all the more. The thirst for infinity can be deceptive, however, as some men tempt themselves with the idea that they can enlarge their own selves to an unlimited extent.

But humans do not relate to God on an equal footing. It was not our expressions of love that made God into many Persons, further increasing the extent of love, the thirst for it, and the understanding of its riches. God does not need our love in the same way that we need His. And this is a result of the limited nature of humans. This is why we are helped to grow in love's infinity and in the joy that comes from loving our fellow men more and more, in the joy that comes from loving others more and more. Still, however many people we love, none of them can truly satisfy us, and none can assure us eternal beatitude, for they cannot open us up to an infinite love. Like us, they remain thirsty for a loving relationship with the Triune God.

Chapter 3

Perfect Love

No conscious being exists except in hypostases or persons: the divine essence in three Persons, the human in many persons. Otherwise neither God nor humans would fulfill the destiny of loving existence and, through this, achieve eternal happiness.

If the divine being were in a single person, it would not be good or loving from eternity, which would mean that it was not divine. But if it were in many persons who were deserving and capable of infinite love, their value would be relativized, and this crowd of people would not be divine either. The divine essence is only divine when hypostasized in three Persons, because these three have a value and a relationship between Them that deserves and is capable of absolute love. And They are like this because each is present in the other, such that God in His entirety can be seen in each, and They are not three separate gods. In response to the idea that God cannot therefore be a single person, we say the following, basing ourselves on the Holy Fathers: A monopersonal god would be neither a person nor God. He would lack perfection, for his omnipotence would not be united with goodness or with love. Would it even still be omnipotence once he became a despot who was incapable of loving relationship with other forms of existence? In this case, what would lead him to create another form of existence from nothing, and would he even be able to create? For why would he want to commune with an existence created in time? A monopersonal god would be like an impersonal essence subordinated to laws of evolution or emanation, laws inexplicable in their origin or their results.

This is why the Holy Fathers fought so strongly against the Arian and Pneumatomachian heresies, which negated the divinity of the Son and of the Holy Spirit, and which, under the pretext of rejecting polytheism, declared that the Son and the Holy Spirit were creatures, or, more precisely, the first among the creatures. St. Athanasius says, "But to say of the Son, 'He might not have been,' is an irreligious presumption reaching even to the Essence of the Father, as if what is His own might not have been. For it is the same as saying, 'The Father might not have been good.' And as the Father is always good by nature, so He is always generative by nature; and to say, 'The Father's good pleasure is the Son,' and 'The Word's good pleasure is the Father,' implies, not a precedent will, but genuineness of nature, and propriety and likeness of Essence."[1]

No essence that is not hypostasized as Father begets a Son, making it a Father, but the supreme essence is hypostasized from eternity as the begetting Father and the begotten Son. It is in its nature to be hypostasized like this; it is in its goodness to be eternally Father and Son. It is not possible to think of a divine essence as existing even for a moment before being hypostasized in the Father and in the Son. It is part of its goodness that it is Father from eternity, hypostasized in the Father and in the Son.

St. Basil the Great makes the divine relationship between the Father and the Son a condition of His goodness and power. "What is good is always present with God who is over all, and . . . it is good to be the Father of such a Son . . . so what is good was never absent from Him, nor was it the Father's will to be without the Son, and when He willed He did not lack the power, but having the power and the will to be in the mode in which it seemed good to Him, He also always possessed the Son by reason of His always willing that which is good."[2]

God would not be good and powerful if there were not in Him a person who could show His goodness to another person. In this case, He would no longer be above all, free to show His goodness eternally and unceasingly. In fact, He would be subordinated to laws. A person shows goodness to another most profoundly when one is a Father and the other a Son from and for eternity.

St. Gregory of Nazianzus argued against the affirmations of the same heretics as well as against others who, admitting three Persons in God, professed three separate gods; such a profession gives the same result as professing a multiplicity of persons who interact in the same way that three or more humans relate to each other. He said, "In these [human] cases the universal is only a unity for speculative thought. The individuals are widely separated from one another by time, temperament, and capacity."[3] Affirming the unity of God before the many gods of the Greeks, St. Gregory says,

> We have one God because there is a single Godhead. Though there are three objects of belief, they derive from the single whole and have reference to it. They do not have degrees of being God or degrees of priority over against one another. They are not sundered in will or divided in power. You cannot find there any of the properties inherent in things divisible. It is as if there were a single intermingling of light, which existed in three mutually connected Suns. When we look at the Godhead, the primal cause, the sole sovereignty, we have a mental picture of the single whole, certainly. But when we look at the three in whom the Godhead exists, and at those who derive their timeless and equally glorious being from the primal cause, we have three objects of worship.[4]

St. John of Damascus says the same thing: "It is just like three suns cleaving to each other without separation and giving out light mingled and conjoined into one."[5] Along the same lines, a hymn from the funeral service refers to "the threefold radiance of the one Godhead."[6] In men a common human nature is possessed by many persons through its repetition in each, so it is not fully united in their persons. The nature is not repeated in the divine Persons but is possessed communally in its entirety. St. Basil the Great says that essence is dispersed (διασκεδασμένη) in men. We see the same essence repeated in hypostases, not fully united yet identical in their repetition. This is why people communicate only in part, and they show that their nature is the same when they will things that they have in common as a result of having the same nature. Between human persons sharing the same nature, there exists a space (or other objects) that makes that nature repeat itself, preventing complete communion. The fact that humans are made of both souls and bodies also contributes to this rupture: even if souls could communicate more easily, bodies prevent full communication.

St. Basil says that there is "a certain communion indissoluble and continuous"[7] in the Persons of the Holy Trinity, a communion uninterrupted by discontinuity and infinite in the content that is communicated between the three Persons. The "mind all the while recognizes no void interval wherein it may travel between Father, Son, and Holy Ghost, for there is nothing inserted between Them; nor beyond the divine nature is there anything so subsisting as to be able to divide that nature from itself by the interposition of any foreign matter. Neither is there any vacuum of interval, void of subsistence, which can make a break in the mutual harmony of the divine essence, and solve the continuity by the interjection of emptiness."[8] When we think of the Father as uncircumscribed and uncreated, we think of the Son and of the Holy Spirit in the same way, because the Son and the Holy Spirit cannot be outside this all-encompassing infinity, outside the only uncreated being and outside its praise, wisdom, and omnipotence, but in each can be seen the uninterrupted and undivided communion. In the same way, it is not possible to think of the Father without the Son or the Holy Spirit, understood in Their all-encompassing infinity. "For it is in no wise possible to entertain the idea of severance or division, in such a way as that the Son should be thought of apart from the Father, or the Spirit be disjoined from the Son. But the communion and the distinction apprehended in Them are, in a certain sense, ineffable and inconceivable, the continuity of nature being never rent asunder by the distinction of the hypostases, nor the notes of proper distinction confounded in the community of essence."[9]

St. Athanasius also says, "Yet, in saying that the Son is in Himself, and both lives and exists like the Father, we do not on that account separate Him from the Father, imagining place and interval between their union in the way of bodies. For we believe that they are united with each other without mediation or distance, and that they exist inseparable; all the Father embosoming the Son, and all the Son hanging and adhering to the Father, and alone resting on the Father's breast continually."[10]

Thus God can neither be a single person (for then He would lack the communion of love) nor a multitude of persons. In the latter case, these persons would be circumscribed and would not be able to encompass everything in each person. So we cannot speak of but a single God, but in three Persons. He is one God through the unity of His essence and of the unlimited love that is His through the relationship between the Father and the Son, united in the Holy Spirit. He does not have this quality of being one God in three Persons because each of the Persons is the same. If this were true, we could also say that three human persons are a single man. And what would stop us from considering all men as a single man, or from saying that the three divine Persons are actually three gods?

He is a single God only because the three divine Persons are in a relationship in which each includes the other two according to the special place that He has in His relationships with Them. Among men everyone is, or can be, both a father and a son. No one is linked with others exclusively as a father or a son. In God, only one is the Father. He represents all paternity and only paternity in relation to a unique Son, who represents all sonship and only sonship in relation to the Father. The Holy Spirit represents a special relationship with both. Thus, when we think of Him as Father and call Him Father, He is understood exclusively as

Father, and He is related totally to the Son. And when we think of and name the Son, He is understood as being in a total and exclusive relationship with the Father. In the same way we also understand the Holy Spirit. Although this relationship is so intimate because the unlimited nature of each of the Persons (and the infinite love that They have for each other) brings love to perfection, even in complete unity it does not involve confusing one with the others.

I cannot think and say "Father" without thinking of and seeing the Son in Him. Thus, I cannot say "the Father" or "the Son of God" without seeing the Son or the Spirit as the same God. The quality of being father of a single son, and only father, presents the Father as the unique, unseen one. What we see is the love of the Father for the Son. The Father is not a Person except insofar as He is the one who loves the Son as a father, so it is not possible to call Him God without seeing the Son united with Him as God. And the Son is only a Son, and the only loving Son of the Father, and thus it is not possible to think of the Son and to call Him Son, as God, without seeing in Him God the Father as well.

A man is the father of a son, or of many sons, but he is also the son of a father. The love of a human son does not unite him completely and exclusively with his father, nor with his own son. But he is united with each of them, or with all of the sons that he has. I do not see in any man only a son, but also something else. Nor in his father do I see only a father, not to speak of his ancestors, his grandchildren, and his brothers. He is not united exclusively and completely with any of these.

In God only one Person has the affection of a Father for all eternity toward an only Son, and another Person has only the affection of a Son for all eternity toward a single Father. They are coeternal Persons found in full communion. They also reveal Themselves like this to the world that They decided to create. The Father cannot but think of and have in Himself an exclusive feeling of love toward the Son and cannot but will for us to think of His Son as united with Him, as united in the praise due to Him as God. As much as He is God, so too is the Son, and vice versa. He does not want me to say, "You are God, but He is not God." He wants me to say, "You are God together with Him. You are both deserving of the same praise as the same God. If You were not the Father of the Son of God, You would not be God. You are God because Your Son is God. You are together God."

Being only Father, and the Father of an only Son, He wants us to think of Him only as united with the Son. He wants nothing but to have the Son with Him, in all His thoughts and feelings, in His whole existence. He does not want not to feel alone in His divinity, and for this very reason He maintains His quality as Father, distinct from the Son, because He alone has the Son and only one Son. The unity of the Father and the Son must be thought of even more deeply: the Father does not want to miss out on experiencing the Son's love for Him, so He unites His feelings as Father toward the Son with the experience of the Son's love for Him, without thereby confusing Himself with the Son. The Father experiences the Son's feelings toward Him as a subject, without becoming confused with the Son. We see the unconfused unity of the Father with the Son in this relationship. And who has not himself felt the very feeling that the Son has for the Father?

We experience this fact even in our relationships among each other, so how could it not be endlessly more intense in the relationships between the divine Persons? And how could this not oblige us to consider the Father and the Son and the Holy Spirit as one God? And when we call the Father God, should we not see in His divinity both the Son and the Holy Spirit as God too, without imagining three gods but also without confusing Them as Persons? We find three Persons together expressing the unrepeated essence in their relationships as Father, Son, and Holy Spirit without being mixed. Each Person bears the entire divine essence unrepeated, so each is fully God, without splitting the essence but also without being confused with the other two. Jesus Christ says these things in many ways, especially in the Gospel of John. For example, when answering Philip's request, "Lord, show us the Father," He says, "He who has seen Me has seen the Father. . . . Do you not believe that I am in the Father, and the Father in Me? The words that I speak to you I do not speak on My own authority; but the Father who dwells in Me does the works. Believe Me that I am in the Father and the Father in Me" (John 14:8–11).

We too live this phenomenon in part, but we are limited, dependent, created beings, and we cannot fully appreciate infinity. When a child speaks, he senses that his mother is speaking too, through him. And he is not the only one who senses this. Those who know both the child and his mother notice it too. People who are close to one another never speak in isolation. Even their actions happen in a sort of communion. A father sees himself in the worthy acts of his son. But an earthly father, being the father of many sons, sees aspects of himself in each of them, and does not see himself completely in any of them. Even if he is the father of only one son, he has the ability to have more sons, and so he will never see himself completely in any of them.

Let us explore the idea of a single God in three Persons more deeply. A person must have an "I" and a "Thou," so as to communicate with others, and a "Him" who can unite them in the interests of a third person. A person must speak with another, and the most interesting and unifying thing is to speak about a third, so that each feels happy. In God each of these three Persons, encompassing all unlimited essence, does not need to be many persons in order to communicate a greater portion of essence. The most loving relationship between an "I" and a "Thou" takes place when one is a father of the other, and only a father, of an only son. If this father were the real or possible father of other sons, and if he had the quality of being a son alongside that of being a father; or if the son were himself the father of other sons, and not only the son of a father but also of a mother, then the love between them would not have all of the being and all of the intensity of the love between one who is exclusively a Father and one who is exclusively a Son.

But if these two did not have a third whom They could love together and who was just as unlimited and exclusive as They were, something that could unite them in a different way would be missing. But this third cannot be a begetter of the Son together with the Father, nor begotten of the Father together with the Son. He cannot be another Son of the Father, nor another Father of the Son. Instead, He is someone who represents the attentions (or the love) of the Father for the Son and the response of the Son in love, as Son, to the Father. He unites both through the reciprocal attention that increases the love between Them, a love that strengthens Them in their qualities as Father and as Son. He proceeds from the Father toward the Son, with the Father's affection, and, arriving at the Son, He returns the Son's affection to the Father. This unites Them all completely in essence and in love, making each fully God, but not three gods, because They are not separated in any way in essence and love.

Several texts from St. Gregory of Nazianzus strengthen this teaching that God is one, although in three Persons, and that each is fully God without there being three gods. Addressing himself to those who affirm that if there were three divine Persons there would be three gods, St. Gregory says,

> But what is our case, our battle, against both parties alike? We have one God because there is a single Godhead. Though there are three objects of belief, they derive from the single whole and have reference to it. They do not have degrees of being God or degrees of priority over against one another. They are not sundered in will or divided in power. You cannot find there any of the properties inherent in things divisible. . . . It is as if there were a single intermingling of light, which existed in three mutually connected Suns. When we look at the Godhead, the primal cause, the sole sovereignty, we have a mental picture of the single whole, certainly. But when we look at the three in whom the Godhead exists, and at those who derive their timeless and equally glorious being from the primal cause, we have three objects of worship.[11]

His opponents asked him, "Do not non-Christians too . . . hold to a single Godhead, and do not we also hold to a single humanity, the whole human race? Nonetheless they think that there is plurality of gods and not just one, in the way that there is a plurality of men."[12] St. Gregory the Theologian responded,

> In these cases the universal is only a unity for speculative thought. The individuals are widely separated from one another by time, temperament, and capacity. We human beings are not merely composite; we are mutually opposed and inconsistent even with ourselves. We do not stay exactly the same for one day, let alone a lifetime. In our bodies and in our souls we are ever fluctuating, ever changing. I do not know whether this is true of angels and of all that exalted nature which comes next after the Trinity, or not. They, though, are not composite, and by their nearness to the crown of beauty are more firmly fixed in their relation to beauty than we are.[13]

The three divine Persons are one God because each presents the unique divine essence in a different mode, and thus They are integrated in a different way than humans are. They are not more or less uniform persons, like humans are, which makes us less integrated. The differences are greater in God, and therefore They do not repeat the essence in Themselves, but each represents the entire essence, only differently. Therefore the Persons integrate more fully, being an integration of three roles of the same unrepeated essence.

Thus each of the three Persons has the other two completely in Himself. The essence, being unlimited, does not repeat itself, but its three Persons are not confused, each using all of the power of the essence in a different way and in a reciprocal communication. Among humans there is communication both physically and spiritually between people who are close to each other, who have the same nature but in a repeated manner, as between nodes that are connected by various threads. Sometimes there are so many threads connecting two people that one's life is lived almost identically with the other one. But every human person cannot live this unity with all others because of the distance between them. In the future life, where those who are in Christ will have a fully developed knowledge of everything, human persons will be united more like the way in which the persons of the Trinity are united. All will be united in the Son with the Father through the Holy Spirit, but not through the same relationships that the divine persons have.

In the earthly life people are not linked by a certain number of threads, but only by the nature that is repeated from another person, as a node radiating out into another. There are many such nodes, some with more connections than others. And the less a person is related through this nature with the essence that is repeated in another person, the more spiritually dead he is. The mode in which the Holy Trinity is united is thus the origin and the eternal helper in creating unity between conscious things.

Chapter 4

Distinct Yet Uninterrupted

The divine essence subsists from eternity, or without a beginning, in three Persons: in the unbegotten Father, in the Son begotten of the Father, and in the Holy Spirit who proceeds from the Father toward the Son. One is not prior to any of the others; there was not one impersonal divine essence before They began to subsist in three Persons. Moreover, the unbegottenness of the Father, the begottenness of the Son, and the proceeding of the Spirit from the Father do not occur successively. In the first prayer of St. Basil the Great for before Holy Communion, one says to the Son, "O Sovereign Lord Jesus Christ our God, source of life and immortality . . . the equally everlasting and co-eternal Son of the eternal Father."[1] One and the same divine nature is in the eternally unbegotten Father, is eternally begotten in the Son, and eternally proceeds in the Holy Spirit. Being unlimited, it does not double or become whole as a result of this process. Instead, the Father has this nature from eternity in an unbegotten way, the Son has it by being eternally begotten of the Father, and the Holy Spirit has it by proceeding eternally from the Father toward the Son. Thus the essence is begotten and proceeds only because it is in the Father, and it is only unbegotten because it is in the Father from eternity. If the essence had been unbegotten in itself, it would also have had to give birth to itself, existing in itself, so there would be an evolution from the state of being an impersonal essence to that of being in three Persons. From eternity the divine essence did not exist in any other way except in the persons of the unbegotten Father, the begotten Son, and the proceeding Spirit.

In the Father the single essence has the quality of being unbegotten for all eternity, but also that of being begetter and processor. In the Son it eternally has the quality of being begotten, and in the Spirit the quality of proceeding. So it does not pass in time from the quality of being unbegotten to that of being begotten and proceeding, from the quality of the Father's essence to those of the Son and Holy Spirit. Instead, it exists from eternity in an unbegotten Person who is also a begetting and processing Father, in the begotten Person of the Son, and in the proceeding Person of the Holy Spirit. All three Persons exist from eternity and do not appear one after the other. Therefore, each of the Persons is in the other two from eternity, not flowing from the Father to the Son and the Holy Spirit in a pantheistic manner according to some law of emanation. Neither did They appear one at a time through acts of will. In this case, we would think of the Father as being temporally prior to the other two, which would reduce God to a monopersonal being, some sort of primary substance with its own laws of development. They could not even have been produced by the combined will of all three. Again, that would involve a law within a primary substance that was later hypostasized in three Persons. They do, however, exist from eternity in a real love that has no beginning. The entire divine nature has been contained in all three Persons from the "moment" it existed in a conscious manner, which is to say, from eternity. The eternal and free mode in which the three divine Persons exist is manifested in Their goodness, such that by existing from eternity the divine Persons show that love has no beginning or cause. It moves from the Father toward the Son and then returns to the Father as the response of the Son. There is no love deeper and purer than that between Father and Son, especially when one is wholly a Father and the other only a Son. A person shows the deepest love when he gives it as a father, and the most complete response is given by one who is a son and nothing but a son. Thus the first Person of the Trinity is unbegotten, manifesting His Personhood by begetting another. And if supreme existence is supreme goodness, it does not flow without volition, but is the free and whole offering of a being who has not received anything. It is a gift whose Giver cannot fail to experience joy in response to the love that is given. He who loves in this way gives completely and receives a loving response to His gift.

If there were no unbegotten Person, there would also be none who was Father from beginning to end. And where would the endless process of begetting end? The union between the eternity and the perfection of the divine Persons is clear. Wanting to give His whole unbegotten Person from eternity, the first Person begat another, in eternity, to whom He gives. Precisely because He gives all of Himself, He is in the other and the other in Him. Eternally being the ultimate origin of all existence, or of all goodness, He gives everything to another Person who is consequently equal to and completely united with Him. This perfect combination of goodness makes the first Person the origin of the others, who receive all of His goodness so that He might take joy in their responses to His giving of His own being. The Eternal One begets the Firstborn, giving all of Himself so that the latter, filling Himself with the unending goodness that He receives, might offer that goodness, together with all His thanks, back to the Unbegotten One.

As people, we also experience the fact that the more we give to others, the richer we become. Giving Himself entirely, the Father begets the one who receives Him so as to receive His gift in return. He also offers the Holy Spirit to the Begotten One as another proof of His love—not as a brother to the Son, but as the one who becomes and the one to whom He shows His love, so as to produce a loving thankfulness within Him.

St. Gregory of Nazianzus puts it this way:

> Though there is numerical distinction, there is no division in the substance. For this reason, a one eternally changes to a two and stops at three—meaning

> the Father, the Son, and the Holy Spirit. In a serene, non-temporal, incorporeal way, the Father is parent of the "offspring" and originator of the "emanation"—or whatever name one can apply when one has entirely extrapolated from things visible. We shall not venture, as a non-Christian philosopher rashly did, to talk of an "overflowing of goodness," "as though a bowl had overflowed"—these were the plain terms he used in his disquisition on primary and secondary causes [cf. Plotinus, *Enneads* 5.2]. We ought never to introduce the notion of involuntary generation (in the sense of some sort of unrestrained natural secretion), which is completely out of keeping with ideas about the Godhead. This is why we limit ourselves to Christian terms and speak of "the Ingenerate," "the Begotten," and (as God the Word himself does in one passage) "what Proceeds from the Father" [John 15:26]. *So when did these last two originate?* They transcend "whenness," but if I *must* give a naive answer—when the Father did. *When was that?* There has not been a "when" when the Father has not been in existence.[2]

If existence is of itself from eternity, it cannot be anything but supreme goodness; it could not have been born somehow, nor could it be unbegetting. It must give completely of itself. But because this existence, identical with unlimited goodness, cannot multiply, its giving and receiving is not a multiplication but an act that causes the second and the third consciousnesses to live by giving and receiving all of the infinity that pertains to this unlimited goodness or existence.

Existence that is conscious of itself from eternity, having in itself goodness that is uncaused by anyone, cannot but be fecund. But fecundity is not about the infinite production of essences, but about the capacity to beget another consciousness, or two other consciousnesses, that can enjoy this goodness. At its base, goodness must be enjoyed together by several conscious beings—in particular, by three, for more would relativize it. Being generative, conscious existence has the capacity and drive to beget other conscious beings to whom it can give everything that it has.

This is why the Fathers saw the relationship between the Father and the Son as a relationship between the Mind and Reason, or as a tripersonal relationship that was fulfilled in the Person of the Father. We could say that this relationship is a sort of self-understanding of being in itself, which takes on a tripersonal character. In its self-consciousness, being in itself (which is complete) has its image, which cannot be devoid of reality, for an image that is simply imaginary would not give real joy. But this image cannot be a separate reality. In Reason (in the Logos) the supreme Mind discovers itself completely, taking joy in itself and in the entire content of its infinity. Reason is an act of the mind, or of the thinking subject. In Reason the intelligence of the supreme subject thinks of itself.

A solitary being cannot even be human, let alone God. Its light and joy exist only in communion with other conscious beings. However alone I might be, I see myself as if I were another person. I talk to myself, I take joy in myself, I rouse myself, I correct myself. In God this conversation of the Father with the Son is only positive, involving only love and joy. God does not correct Himself in the Person of the Son, but takes joy in Himself.

Thus the Evangelist John spoke of a personal Word of God who has no beginning in the way that one speaks about a person. "In the beginning was the Word, and the Word was with God, and the Word was God" (John 1:1). The Word that the Father hears from His Son is truly that of another Person, but of a Person who is in complete accord with Him. That Person speaks and responds as His personified Word. If the Father did not speak with another Person, that Person would not exist. And as the Father speaks it, the Word that He utters is personified, becoming a distinct Person who answers Him, revealing the personal character assumed by the Father's Word. The life of God as joyful love is revealed in the Father's conversation with the Word. This conversation sheds a light that is full of sense and reason onto divine existence. The Son of God is called the Word or Reason begotten of the Father because He includes in His Person the one who holds the reason according to which all created things were patterned. This is the sense in which we can understand the words of St. Maximus the Confessor: "The head of Christ, of unfathomable, mysterious Reason, is the Mind, raised absolutely and infinitely over all things and in all ways. This is who Christ, understood spiritually as the Mind's Reason, makes known to the faithful."[3]

St. Maximus' words show that there is not a complete separation between the created world and the God who has a Son. God gave the created world rationality according to the pattern of His Son. Humans too are unities of intelligences, or incorporated words, made to know God the Father through the Son and, through words, to be united with the Word of the Father. The intelligences of this world are created to live together in God-given harmony. They move toward God, so they are not enemies of God's Word and of love. This is said more precisely in one of St. Maximus' scholia: "Because He is together with Reason, which is the creator of everything, one thinks of the Mind, to which Reason reports as to its cause. This is known as the Father, or the head of Christ, because as the Mind He begets Reason."[4]

As Mind, the Father is the head of Reason, in which all created intelligences dwell harmoniously. If we use our reason properly, we discover in it the harmony of all the world's intelligences, the explanation of which we find in their unity in the Son and, by extension, in their ultimate point of origin in the Father. Intelligences partake of a unity that is higher than they are. The intelligence of one person tries to understand first that of another and then all of the world's intelligences, each of which exists independently from that thinking being. Intelligences communicate to others through words as they search for an ever more profound, more universal, and more enlightening understanding of a world whose origin is beyond them. The divine Reason is the only one that can explain the world to us, and in this sense it is the intelligence of the world, even though it is also superior to this intelligence.

Divine Reason is found in the world, yet it surpasses the world. St. Maximus the Confessor explains the link between divine Reason and the world in the following manner: "He who mysteriously received, through the negation of his understanding of created things, an unmediated vision of that Reason which is above every reason has as his head that completely unique Reason, above and alongside which no other exists. That Reason is the product of a single Mind, toward which it moves, as toward its own head, giving life to the mind that follows it according to the Spirit, which is one with it."[5]

The human mind seeks after the supreme Reason because in it we find the meaning of life and of all things. There is a link between reason and life. But true life does not exist without love, which is harmony between persons and whose model and ultimate wellspring is God. Its meaning is identical with the supreme Mind. From it and to it, as from the Father and to the Father, or toward the origin of all things, is the Reason according to which everything is created. We climb toward the Father through that reason which gathers created intelligences together and points them toward the supreme Reason, which, as their cause, explains everything. And through this Reason we come closer to the meaning of all things, which no longer need any other explanation, for it illuminates everything in itself.

"The head of that Reason which is above all things . . . is the uncaused Mind, thought of together with the Reason whose cause it is. For he who sees Reason through faith sees the Mind together with it, which begets Reason outside of time, being found in Reason according to its being."[6] The supreme Reason that explains everything, although it is above our powers of understanding, can nonetheless be touched through faith. There is no opposition between faith and reason. Therefore, having reached this Reason, I have also mysteriously reached the supreme Mind, as the meaning of everything. The ultimate meaning of things can only be found in God. He is uncaused by anything and is the origin of all things through the Son, through Reason. The supreme Meaning is higher than any reasoning because it has no cause. It is the ultimate cause of all rational things. This inexplicable supreme Meaning is the same as the supreme uncaused Subject. He cannot take joy completely in Himself if He does not understand Himself through another. That other is His Reason. The two of them remain in eternal love, or communion, out of which flow the rationality, love, and harmony of all things.

If, through an action of the mind or of the intelligence, the Father discovers Himself as a rational being—as Logos—and if this is His real image, then through His feelings (through the Spirit) He loves this image of Himself. His Son, the Word or supreme Reason, is the product of the Father's thinking about Himself, and the Holy Spirit, as the Father's love for His image, is the product of His feelings or of His "heart." The Son is the doubling of what is thought of by the Father; He is His ontological image. The Spirit is the projection of His love toward this ontological image of Himself.

St. Basil the Great also sees in the name "the Word" the entire thinking of God the Father about Himself. St. Basil asks himself, "Why is He called 'the Word'?" and answers, "In order to show that He comes from the Mind." And later he continues,

> Because He is the image of the one who has begotten Him, revealing and completing the latter in Himself. His existence is complete in itself, but without introducing a separation into the one who brought Him into being, just as our words reveal our thoughts in their entirety. . . . Thus John called Him "the Word" so as to show His being begotten of the Father, to theologize the perfect being of the Son, and to show the Son's relationship with the Father outside of time. Our words proceed from our minds in the same way, without consuming them. They are not separated from the mind. They do not share in it or flow from it, but the mind generates complete words while remaining essentially whole. Moreover, words contain all of the power of the mind that produces them.[7]

When the Evangelist says, "And the Word was with God, and the Word was God. . . . All things were made through Him" (John 1:1, 3), he shows the personal character of the Word as one that is strictly united with the Father. Moreover, he shows that the Father revealed Himself first and foremost through the Son. In the Son, the Father began a dialogue with Himself in eternity, as with another Person to whom He was closely bound. Thus the text "All things were made through Him" also shows that in God the Word is an omnipotent power that brings everything into existence out of nothing, in communion with the Father and out of His goodwill. God sustains everything through His Word, who is full of power. The Word is free with regard to created things, but they do not exist without Him and without the loving communion between the Father and the Son. They did not come into being through involuntary evolution, but through the free Word and the goodwill of the Father, who used Him to create all things. The Word shows us both the eternal communion that He has with the Father and the power of the Father to use Him freely to create, sustain, and draw conscious beings to Him.

In the Word people meet each other and the Word of God. John the Evangelist uses the name "the Word" to show us not only the interpersonal nature of the divinity but also the will and power of God to meet humans and to help them meet each other. For God placed the power and the injunction of words in each one of us so that we might have communion with each other and with the divine Word.

Another meaning of "In the beginning was the Word" is that the Son of God has conversed with His Father for eternity. For He "was" when there occurred a "beginning" in general; that is, He was there before any beginning, before anything come into existence in time. He was before time. He is from eternity. For otherwise everything would not have been created through Him. Purely and simply, He has no beginning, for He is begotten of the Father. He was begotten before time, just as the Father existed before time. One is unbegotten, the other begotten, such that the Son has the Unbegotten One as His Father, but because there was no time when God was not Father, so too there was no time when

He did not have a Son. It follows from the eternity of God that He is the ultimate origin not only of unconscious and unimportant things, but also of a Subject who is equal to Himself in its infinity and unlimitedness. It is an eternal communion, or a love that is full of joy and life from eternity.

The idea of the "word" as a meeting between persons, as the eternal communion of the Word with the Father, is seen in the Romanian word for interpersonal communication, for speech. In Romanian the word *cuvânt* indicates not only the expressing of someone's thought but also the "arriving at a place" (*conventus*) of a second person (or more persons). The world was created through the supreme and free *conventus*, though a *conventus* of the love of the Father and the Son. This eliminates any pantheism in explanations of the world. The divine Word shows that even after they have been created, humans can refuse to respond positively to the will of the Son of God. For the word is a free act, used by any created person as he wishes, not only for good. In giving humans words, God respects their liberty. Just as He speaks freely when He creates everything for good purposes, He gives them the power to use words not only to unite themselves to each other and to God through love, but also against His wishes, while still remaining linked, through their contradictory word, with their brethren and with God.

Chapter 5

The Love of a Son

If there were no eternal relationship in God between the Father and the Son, then there would be no basis for bringing conscious beings into existence, for calling them forever into the blessed state of brotherhood with the Son. They are nourished by the everlasting relationship of the Son with the Father. No higher destiny is conceivable for humanity. Precisely because He is a Father and has a Son from eternity, God created a category of beings toward whom He could show a love like the one that exists between Him and His Son. He created beings whom He could raise up to love the Father as the Son does, to love the Son as a brother, and to love each other as brethren. For this reason the Son was the most closely involved in the creation of humans and their world, and so, when they fell away from the purpose for which they were created, He became human Himself. Christ offers us Himself as our model and empowers us to love God and each other. There can be no supreme and eternal being that can be taken as a higher model and goal than such a God.

The Church Fathers say that if there were no Son of God who shared His essence with the Father, the Father would have had no reason to create humans as children in the likeness of the only begotten Son, who could love them and they Him. Without this Son there would have been no one who, out of love for the Father, would desire to create other beings who could love the Father just as he did. It would have been as if God were not all-powerful. Separated from humans, He as an essence would have been subordinated to laws from which He had no escape. Without a God who was both Father and Son (and Holy Spirit), nothing would have existed except the god pantheists imagine: an essence out of which everything evolves according to endless, blind laws. When men refused to respond to God's love by loving Him in return, the Son entrusted the Father with the task of making Him human. As a man He could show men what it looked like for humans to love God, and He could give them the ability to do so themselves.

But how was it possible for humans to not respond to the love of God, and to not love each other? And how, by not loving, did they become enslaved and dead, while their model, the only begotten Son of God, loved the Father perfectly? This painful part of human history can be explained through the fact that men could not be brought into existence as infinite, godly beings, but only as circumscribed beings. They received bodies to help them. With bodies, men could help each other and could sanctify both their bodies and the whole universe. They were also created as free beings. The only begotten Son, having in Himself the infinite being of the Father, could help to raise them once again to likeness with God. Loving the Father in His very being, from eternity, the Son contained this salvific gift in Himself from the beginning.

God asked humans to respond to His love by loving Him and each other out of their own free will. In their free will, they as circumscribed beings had the urge to extend themselves. But man could easily be tempted to think that he had to fight for his own subjectivity so as to enlarge his life, and thus to care less for God and others. He might even fight with others, each trying to take things that might benefit him alone. Thus men no longer valued loving God and others, and they abandoned reason, which would have shown them that they could expand only through collaboration with each other. Cooperation comes through faith in God, who, as the Maker of all, requires unity in love. Their reason had united them to the Reason of God—His Word, the Logos—but they replaced it with egoistic, individualistic speculation, thereby creating a battle that repeats inside each and every person.

St. Maximus the Confessor developed this idea extensively in his *Letter on Love, to John the Cubicularius*. He described how humans chose to hate, instead of moving toward each other in love and considering others as equal to themselves, as the Holy Trinity does. They chose to hate each other and to increase the fighting among themselves; they sustained within the framework of the one nature, repeated in all of them, the power to tear each other apart. Without faith in God, men cannot overcome the temptation to seek infinity within their own beings. Such a victory is only possible if we rely on the only one who can bring unity between Himself and us through love. We can achieve natural unity among human beings only by being united with God. The natural human state can only exist when there is unity among different persons, which comes through reciprocal love and through unity with God. The Son of God came as a man to convince us and to give us the grace—His power—to conquer our egoistic reasoning, which leads us into an unnatural battle with ourselves and with God. Christ uses our reasoning to convince us to act according to our nature. Just as we all have a single nature, so we all can have a single reasoning and a single will with God among us. There will be no separation from God or between us when we choose to govern our lives by the law inscribed in our restored nature through the law of grace. But those who have not first united themselves with God through wisdom and right thinking can never freely agree among themselves.

> For since the deceitful devil at the beginning contrived by guile to attack humankind through his self-love, deceiving him through pleasure, he has separated us in our inclinations from God and from one another, and turned us away from rectitude. He has divided nature at the level of mode of existence, fragmenting it into a multitude of opinions and imaginations. He has set up the means through which each vice may be discovered,

> and with time established a law, to which all our powers are devoted, introducing into everything a wicked support for the continuance of vice—namely, irreconcilable inclinations. By this he has prevailed on humankind to turn from the natural movement he once had and to move his longing from what is permitted to what is forbidden. . . . For out of ignorance concerning God there arises self-love. And out of this comes tyranny towards one's kin. . . . For reason, instead of being ignorant, ought to be moved through knowledge to seek solely after God. . . . And the divine and blessed love, which is fashioned from these and through which these came to be, will embrace God and manifest the one who loves God to be God himself.[1]

For love, unlike the reasoning of self-love, "gathers together what has been separated, once again fashioning the human being in accordance with a single meaning and mode. It levels off and makes equal any inequality of difference in inclination in anything, or rather binds it to that praiseworthy inequality, by which each is so drawn to his neighbor in preference to himself and so honours him before himself, that he is eager to spurn any obstacle in his desire to excel."[2] And "each is in each, and all in all, or rather in God and in others."[3] And man is led toward God, "having relinquished the individuality of what divides and is divided, no longer leading another human being different from himself, but knowing all as one and one as all. . . . Looking to the utterly singular reason [*logos*], by which we have established that God is certainly manifest, and through which God is set forth as good, making the creatures his own, since creation cannot know God from himself, as he is in himself."[4]

Through Christ we become like the Trinity in valuing others as we value ourselves. The Father does not distance Himself from the Son and the Holy Spirit, and They do not think about separating Themselves from the Father. Rather, each sees Himself in the other and is more preoccupied with the other's good than with His own. This is what love feels like: it unites, but without confusing one person with another. Valuing the other more than yourself, you do not focus on what separates you from him. Instead, you find your greatest joy in discovering that his life is oriented toward yours. This is the Reason (the Word) who unites us, and in Him we live the supreme Sense of our existence (the Father). But this goal was first realized by the Son, whose life as a man shows us the way we need to follow and gives us the strength to do so.

Along with His human body, Christ took on those passions that entered our flesh when we separated ourselves from God and each other. But by accepting only the passions of suffering, and not those of pleasure, He overcame them. Submitting even to death, which oppressed us through our own free will, He conquered it. In doing so, He gave us the power to defeat death if we unite ourselves with Him through faith and if we separate ourselves as much as possible from the passions of pleasure and from the guilt that they bring with them. We can see the love of the Son of God become man in His suffering for us, to the point of death on the cross. He is the best brother to us because He shows us the power of God working through His love. If we too renounce egoistic passions and accept sufferings for our egoistic sins, we show our love for God, who, incarnate as a man, received death to conquer them.

In Christ we see how God overcame death by uniting Himself with humanity through love. Rather than arbitrarily using His omnipotence to defeat death, He made us beloved by God and capable of receiving His power so that we too can defeat death through His love. Love defeats death in creation because it is united with the power of God. If in His omnipotence God created the world through love, it is also because of love that He chose to use material beings to bring creation back to life. The Son of God wants to dialogue in a body with other corporeal beings. Christ took a body, showing that even as God He can speak with men in a body that has eternal life. He resurrected the body that He had made His own so as to resurrect others through Himself. For this to happen it was necessary for humans to respond to the love of their Creator, who desired to give them eternal life. He wanted to win the love of ordinary men through His body so that they might be resurrected through His omnipotence. Omnipotence alone has no reason to resurrect men, who are changed only thanks to the dialogue of love. Love puts omnipotence in motion. One could even say that omnipotence is contained within love: it is not possible to think of one without the other. God's love is shown in Christ's suffering for us, as He helps us to endure suffering, subduing egoistic pleasure by suffering for God.

Where there is love, there is also the power to conquer the effects of evil, effects that diminish our existence. Where there is no love, there is powerlessness, or poverty of life. In short, there is spiritual death. In God, love is empowered and united with omnipotence so that perfect existence becomes one in which nothing is felt to be lacking. But love is not possible in a monopersonal existence. Love implies communion with others. It means orienting myself toward another, and thereby displaying my power. On the other hand, love overcomes all laws of necessity. God does not live subordinated to laws, forced to limit evil, because He Himself is complete goodness living in the greatest freedom. He created men as circumscribed beings and called them to ascend through communion among themselves and with Him. The path was marked for them, and they were helped by laws inscribed both on tablets and in nature. Beyond explicit divine commandments, humans also had to follow natural laws in order to fulfill the law of goodness. But by not listening to God and by disobeying His commandments, men turned those commandments into laws that bring suffering and, eventually, death. Trying to escape from them, men followed their desires, which in turn became like oppressive laws for them.

Taking a human body, the Son of God overcame the dominion of these laws without letting Himself be led into breaking them, all the while patiently enduring punitive suffering according to the laws of goodness. Through His innocence and endurance, and with the great power of human love, He raised His body above those laws. If men unite themselves with Christ through faith, they too can defeat these laws while they live on earth. But they will overcome them completely when they are resurrected. Then love, which is an extension of God for eternity, will raise them up above all laws. They will be kings in the kingdom that Christ has prepared for them, a kingdom that He helps them advance toward through His Church. In their preparation for the kingdom of free, perfect love, they are helped by the Holy Spirit of Christ. The rulers of this kingdom will be our Father, our Brother, and His Spirit, who are present in us. Thus we will also rule, for we are in Them.

In fact, all the teaching and works of Christ are aimed at winning people for the kingdom of God. St. Matthew writes in his Gospel about the beginning of Christ's proclamation: "From that time Jesus began to preach and to say, 'Repent, for the kingdom of heaven is at hand'" (Matt 4:17). And then he says, "And Jesus went about all Galilee, teaching in their synagogues, preaching the gospel of the kingdom" (Matt 4:23). Christ teaches us to pray to God, to call Him Father and ask, "Your kingdom come." In the Beatitudes He promises the poor in spirit and those who are persecuted for righteousness' sake that theirs is the kingdom of heaven. In the Sermon on the Mount He tells men, "Seek first the kingdom of God and His righteousness, and all these things shall be added to you" (Matt 6:33). This verse shows how we should prepare for the kingdom of heaven. In the Sermon on the Mount, in which He gives all the commands of love to mankind, the Savior says, "Whoever therefore breaks one of the least of these commandments, and teaches men so, shall be called least in the kingdom of heaven; but whoever does and teaches them, he shall be called great in the kingdom of heaven" (Matt 5:19). The commandments that He asks us to keep are those of love, of mercy, and of forgiving to the extent of turning the other cheek when someone slaps you. Dominion in the kingdom of heaven is not for the proud but for the humble: "Assuredly, I say to you, unless you are converted and become as little children, you will by no means enter the kingdom of heaven" (Matt 18:3). In order to be a part of this kingdom, we must be "children of our Father in heaven," together with His Son, who humbled Himself in love to the point of taking the form of a man. The children of our heavenly Father bless those who curse them and love their enemies (Matt 5:44–45).

If dominion in this kingdom belongs to the Trinity, humans cannot participate in the kingdom without uniting themselves with it and living, through its power, in community with other men. Thus he who humbles himself and becomes like a little child will enter into the kingdom of heaven (Matt 18:4). Those who escaped from under those burdensome laws that are difficult to fulfill through human power alone become, through love, the rulers of all. On the other hand, those who do the will of the heavenly Father exhibit love, fulfilling all of the commandments of Jesus, following the teaching of the Father, who "makes His sun rise on the evil and on the good, and sends rain on the just and on the unjust" (Matt 5:45).

In these days after Christ has ascended into heaven, it is only through the Holy Spirit that men can prepare themselves to enter this love that overcomes all laws. This was what the Savior meant when He told Nicodemus, "Most assuredly, I say to you, unless one is born of water and the Spirit, he cannot enter the kingdom of God" (John 3:5). As a man, the Son conquered through the Holy Spirit, patiently enduring the weaknesses that sin had brought upon mankind and then overcoming sin's final blow: death. We will see how the Holy Spirit can help us conquer these weaknesses and how He can help men to be resurrected, defeating the laws that sin has brought upon us. First we shall see how Christ—who assumed and bore these weaknesses out of His own free will, not out of necessity—triumphed. In His life acts of power were interspersed with acts of weakness and human suffering, although He sometimes combined both mysteriously. This is a contradictory unity, one that can relate the finite to the infinite because there is a relationship between the finite and the infinite anyway, and the finite can be enlarged to contain the infinite in itself. God deifies that which is human, and man humanizes that which is divine without desanctifying it.

Note the way in which St. Gregory of Nazianzus describes how divinity was united with human weakness in Christ:

He who is presently human was incomposite. He remained what he was; what he was not, he assumed. No "because" is required for his existence in the beginning, for what could account for the existence of God? But later he came into being because of something, namely your salvation, yours, who insult him and despise his Godhead for that very reason, because he took on your thick corporeality. Through the medium of the mind he had dealings with the flesh, being made that God on earth, which is Man: Man and God blended. . . . in order that I might be made God to the same extent that he was made man. He was begotten [Matt 1:16]—yet he was already begotten [Ps 2:7; Acts 13:33; Heb 1:5; 5:5]—of a woman [Gal 4:4]. And yet she was a virgin [Luke 1:34–35; Matt 1:20]. That it was from a woman makes it human, that she was a virgin makes it divine. On earth he has no father [Matt 1:20], but in heaven no mother [Ps 2:7]. All this is part of his Godhead. He was carried in the womb [Luke 1:31], but acknowledged by a prophet as yet unborn himself, who leaped for joy at the presence of the Word for whose sake he had been created [Luke 1:41]. He was wrapped in swaddling bands [Luke 2:7, 12; John 19:40], but at the Resurrection he unloosed the swaddling bands of the grave [John 20:5–7]. He was laid in a manger [Luke 2:7], but was extolled by angels [Luke 2:13–14], disclosed by a star [Matt 2:2] and adored by Magi [Matt 2:11]. . . . He was exiled into Egypt [Matt 2:13–14], but he banished the Egyptian idols. . . . As man he was baptized [Matt 3:16; Luke 3:21], but he absolved sins as God [John 1:29; Matt 9:2]; he needed no purifying rites himself—his purpose was to hallow water. As man he was put to the test [Matt 4:1; Luke 4:2], but as God he came through victorious [Matt 4:11]. . . . He hungered [Matt 4:2; Luke 4:2]—yet he fed thousands [Matt 14:20–21]. He is indeed "living, heavenly bread" [John 6:51].[5]

Chapter 6

INCARNATION

Having created everything through His Word and only begotten Son (John 1:3), God created men as images of His Son so that He might extend His fatherly love to other sons. Those sons do not share the same essence with Him, and therefore they are not sons according to intrinsic laws, for this would relativize the only begotten Son and would subordinate God to laws, thus breaking down the distinction between God and the world. But wanting to give being to all forms of existence, He created and ordered matter such that humans are made of both spirits and bodies. He created matter (and the material world) so that created beings could express their love and be united through it. Matter is nonetheless dependent on the human will to express love, as well as on spiritual strength.

Humans fell from the loving relationship that they had with the Father and the Son because they failed to exercise strength of will over matter. Therefore the Son became a man. He was composed of spirit and matter like us, yet He remained God. He did this with the blessing of the Father, who created man in His image in order to forge an unbreakable union between humanity and God. This action of His shows that matter is capable of being formed, through the Spirit, into a collection of organs through which the riches of spiritual activity can be manifested. The Son of God created just such a composition when He made Himself man. That is to say, He took on a soul and a material body made up of organs, through which He could manifest Himself as God. The Son made the body into an organ of eternal and deified life, freeing this body and soul from death, under whose curse it fell through sin, through a weakness of the spirit. Matter was created by God as fully capable of carrying the divine hypostasis, and thus the Holy Trinity itself.

So as to make this supreme mystery easier to understand, it is better to reflect on the mystery through which the human spirit, created in the image of the Son of God, can give matter a bodily form that can be used to carry out its multiple functions. Matter is not created in order to remain amorphous, or to have only a single form. A Church prayer that we will come back to later speaks about the role of the Holy Spirit in shaping the universe, made up of stars that give light to people on earth through their fiery matter. The psalms often comment on the fact that the entire material universe, with its harmonious order, was created and is sustained by God through His Holy Spirit: "The heavens declare the glory of God; The firmament shows the creation of His hands" (Ps 18:1). The Bible describes the wonders of the universe on a grand scale, as in Psalm 135. The beginning of Genesis tells us that "the Spirit of God was hovering over the face of the water" (Gen 1:2), or that God organized the entire universe so that superior things could make use of inferior things through His Word, which is inseparable from the Holy Spirit.

Certain powers are found even in matter, and these powers contribute to the harmonious organization of the universe according to God's purposes for the human spirit. In this sense, the Apostle Paul says that divine Reason can be seen in the universe and that God used it when He formed and ordered the world. "For since the creation of the world His invisible attributes are clearly seen, being understood by the things that are made, even His eternal power and Godhead" (Rom 1:20).

Thousands of years ago, the Holy Scriptures knew of the wisdom of God that was imprinted upon the universe, but science will not find it in material things any time soon. The Greeks believed that matter is a uniform mass composed of identical atoms. Modern chemistry has only recently discovered the varied number of atoms and the various molecules that are formed as energies bind them together. Modern physics has discovered the various forces found in matter: movement, electricity, heat, atomic energy. How could the riches of the flowers and plants, in which the Savior Himself saw the careful hand of God, have been produced by uniform atoms? "So why do you worry about clothing? Consider the lilies of the field, how they grow . . . even Solomon in all his glory was not arrayed like one of these" (Matt 6:28–29).

Modern astronomy has discovered a great number of heavenly bodies, arrayed in vast planetary systems, each moving around the others, each attracting the other while both still remain distinct bodies. This is the law of gravity, first discovered by Newton. And Planck established the limitations of the material order through quantum theory. It is equally miraculous how the body's organs are arranged out of collections of molecules: the heart, lungs, stomach, and the senses are all joined together in a body, and all serve the conscious purposes of the human subject. Through each of them flows the conscious unity of the same subject.

Who can explain the way that matter can be organized in so many different ways and can be made into the host of things that the human soul imagines, wills, and senses? God must be present together with His handiwork in this marvelous relationship between the human soul and matter, a relationship that corresponds so perfectly to the organization of the body. What a great mystery rests in the power of the soul to locate the understanding of all these things in the eyes, which are specifically designed for this purpose; to express its will through a voice emanating from speech organs; and so forth.

Why could not the Son of God, who created man in His own image, organize and make use of matter in an even more intimate and direct manner, to make a body for Himself? For from where would the soul have the capacity to organize so much complex and interrelated matter in bodily organs if not from the harmonious riches of the rationality of the divine Logos? Is it possible that all this happened accidently, without a purpose or a goal: the integration of the heart with the lungs, the stomach and the liver, all sustaining the life of a conscious soul housed in a body within an entire universe? Does this not prove the existence of a superior rational will, which imagined and organized the reality of the whole world, placing man as its conscious center and directing him, through his desires, toward a relationship with the Creator who is above all things?

A great and wonderful mystery is also seen in the fact that the soul too feels pain (and pleasure) from blows or cuts, or pleasure from caresses, food, or rest in the material body. Taking on a body, the Son of God experienced painful suffering in His body too, suffering that culminated in the nails hammered into this body on the cross. It is not true that the unique hypostasis of Christ sat to one side, not caring about the suffering that He was going through. Thus He raised His material body from the dead, feeling the joy that was transparent in His resurrected body. Mercy is not lacking in the goodness of God, and mercy does not exist without emotions. Just as a mother's soul suffers when her child faces hardships, so too God suffers for men. His Son lives as "the Lamb of God who takes away the sin of the world" (John 1:29), who was sacrificed in place of men for their sins in order to free them from these sins, and with the certainty that the Father would not remain unmoved in the face of His Son's pain.

Of course, the Son of God did not consign Himself to a material body or mingle human deeds with divine ones on a whim. He did this, together with the miracles that He performed in the body, in order to obey the will of God. But the fact that He could organize and work divine purposes through a human body in a pure and marvelous manner shows that He created Himself as a man with a material body, and thus created all matter with the capacity for being filled and used to manifest His divine Person. And He raised men through grace to become sons of His heavenly Father through the fact that He Himself was the only begotten Son of the heavenly Father. If there were no Triune God—a God who was Father, Son, and Holy Spirit—He could not have done this. The raising of man from the prison of his nature is possible thanks to the fact that God exists in Trinity. Otherwise everything would be reduced to an essence of this world, subordinated to laws of an inexplicable origin.

The senses of the material body can entice us into privileging pleasurable feelings over joy in the Spirit of God, who is pure spirit. Only strengthening the ties between the human spirit and God can make the body into a vehicle for pure spiritual joy. The Son of God achieved this because the divine Spirit strengthened His relationship with the human spirit. The fact that man fell from the love of God should not lead us to think that God was unable to make man incapable of such a fall. The fall was possible because man limited the infinite, believing it possible to establish new limits for himself and for the universe. Because human efforts to subordinate matter to the spirit were weak and ineffective, the material body fell into a process of disintegration that ends in death. In taking on a body, the Son of God experienced the sufferings that humans go through in their bodies, but by enduring them without separating Himself from God, He made enduring suffering—and even death—into a demonstration of the Spirit's power. This is how it was possible for Him to raise His body from the dead. He took our sins upon His shoulders, suffering for them even until death, and He thereby conquered this weakening of matter, together with death itself. The human thirst for infinity is fulfilled by God as He draws all forms of being—including those made of both spirit and matter—into His spiritual existence. God desires to see the beauty of the created soul's love for Him. This love is beautiful thanks to the divine power at work in the soul and because of the way in which it is expressed through matter.

The Son's character as Word can also help us understand how humans are raised up through His incarnation. St. John the Evangelist's expression "In the beginning was the Word" means not only that the Son of God is without beginning and is a divine Person like the Father, in loving dialogue with the Father, but also that He is before everything that has a beginning, that all things that have a beginning came into existence through Him, and that all are organized according to His word or reason. All things find harmony inasmuch as their reasons are in Him. Just as the Son—as the Word of the Father—is engaged in an eternal, loving response to the Father, so too are humans, created in His image as words or with words. Therefore, when this human bond with the Father became weak, He who is bonded completely with the Father became a man who could share with them the bond that He has with the Father.

He Himself powerfully experiences within Himself, as the divine Son, this perfect bond with the Father, and He also imprints it upon His humanity. This bond is further extended to include all those who believe in Him as the Son of God. This is how men are brought into the loving relationship of the Trinity. Being included in the Son's bond with the Father, they are also united with each other. Just as the Son experiences His bond with the Father in His Person (which implies that the Son is assured of the esteem and love of the Father and responds with His own loving response), He also offers this bond to men, asking them to take part in the reciprocal giving and receiving of love. This means that each person has in his word a request that includes a declaration of his love for the other and that asks for the other's response. This exchange is based on the way that the incarnate Son declares His love for the Father even in His humanity. This declaration and response would not exist without an interpersonal relationship. And the supreme origin of the offer and response is in the Trinity. The Trinity is the supreme expression of the declaration of love, a declaration beginning in the Father and answered by the Son.

Chapter 7

Three Is Perfection

The highest form of love is revealed to us in the unending love between the one and only Father of a unique Son. This love is shown in its perfection, existing from eternity. Yet throughout eternity the love between the Father and the Son has also been directed toward a third Person who takes joy in the love that each has for the other. The simple fact that there is another Person in addition to the two found in the "I-Thou" relationship adds a new, fruitful note to the love between the two, giving it a new importance. Of course, one could say that because the Father and the Son are both infinite, there is no need for another Person to add something new to the love of one for the other. But this implies that even one Person in the Godhead would, in His infinity, be sufficient for His own happiness. If the infinity of a Person requires a second Person to bring joy to the love of the first, why would not the infinity of Their love, which is the first mode of love, require another Person who adds a new mode to love, increasing the first mode in its infinity? Infinity in itself does not bring joy to love, but showing love before someone else does. Where consciousness is missing, so too is joy. But real joy comes from another consciousness that is attentive to one's own. Even in humans, who are created in God's likeness, we see that a third person—beyond you and I—brings a new and fruitful mode to our love, and hence to our joy. The love between "I" and "Thou," even in infinity, desires to extend itself toward another person. Joy between two people grows when it is joined with the joy of a third, or when the joy of the two lovers lives in the joy that a third person has for them both. Perhaps this is what St. Athanasius of Alexandria meant when he said, "The Lord himself said that the Spirit is a Spirit of Truth and Comfort: this shows that the Trinity is perfected in the Spirit."[1] In this sense, St. Gregory Palamas explains that this quality of the Spirit of truth and wisdom—and I could also add the quality of Comforter—is not only a gift of the Spirit for humans, continuing the work of the Son, but "the beloved Word and Son of the Father also experiences this love towards the Begetter, but he does so inasmuch as he possesses this love as proceeding from the Father together with him and as resting connaturally in him."[2] I will give the context of this quote below (p. 63) in order to show how St. Gregory Palamas sees the Spirit as the one who is necessary for the fullness of love and joy in God. We shall see that two Persons do not exhaust love's possibilities, but that there is need for a third, who is not merely a link, but who is united with the other two.

As humans, we live this fact through the simple linguistic need to add a "Him" to the "I-Thou." We cannot forget a "Him" when we are in an "I-Thou" relationship. Perhaps the more we love each other, the more we will also feel love toward him. We feel the need to be loved by a third and to love a third, and the more we love him together, the more we love one another. The Russian theologian Pavel Florensky explains the truth about the number three in the following manner: "But I will be asked: Why are there precisely three hypostases? I speak of the number 'three' as immanent to the Truth, as inwardly inseparable from the Truth. . . . Only in the unity of Three does each hypostasis receive an absolute affirmation, which establishes this hypostasis as such. Outside the Three, there is not one, there is no Subject of the Truth."[3] If it were only the two of us, we would feel that there was something missing from reality. Even the divine being needs to live in complete thankfulness, in a relationship between three personal consciousnesses.

I do not want to be loved only by one (by "Thou"), however infinite you might be, but I want your love for me to be accompanied by a third (by a "Him"); and you ("Thou") want the same: to have another who loves you together with me. But the third also wants to see us united in love toward him, or in his love toward us. The infinite essence of a person does not satisfy me through its love. I feel that this is not the full reality of love. Love is ultimately based on the consciousness of another person. I see his love in his consciousness, just as he sees my love in mine. The consciousnesses of two people are subjects that give and receive love. And in God, given the infinity of His Persons, there is a single "Him" who completes the love that I await and who satisfies us with His love.

But the third cannot be like the second—He cannot be a Son. That would mean that the Son was not able to attract the full love of the Father. Rather, there must be a Person from another category who, even in the way in which He receives His subsistence from the Father, shows the Father loving the Son and the Son loving the Father. The Spirit unites the Father and the Son ever more closely in this way, which brings Him to be loved by both, and to love both, showing His special love for each in connection with the love that each has for the other, and the special love that each has for Him. He makes the Son to be even more beloved of the Father and the Father to be even more beloved of the Son. Thus the Father does not love the Son except in the Spirit, nor does He love the Spirit except in the Son. In the Spirit the Father loves us as spiritual sons, and the Son loves us as His spiritual brothers.

The Spirit strengthens the unity between the Father and the Son through His love, and They strengthen the unity between Themselves through Their love for Him. It is not possible to go beyond the love between the Father and the Son through the Spirit. Either the Son is seen in the Spirit, or vice versa. The goal is that They might be seen even after the Son is incarnated in us. St. Gregory of Nazianzus says, "From unity is the Trinity, and from Trinity again the unity."[4] Each embraces and frequently discovers not His "I," but the other's. Therefore, all three can be seen in each hypostasis. "You see then," says St. Basil the Great, "that sometimes the Father reveals the Son, and at other times the Son reveals the Father. So the entire Godhead is revealed sometimes in the Father, sometimes in the Son, and sometimes in the Spirit."[5]

Therefore, while the Son was on earth, the Spirit revealed Him especially, and since the Son ascended and was glorified, He has revealed the Spirit. The Son discloses the Spirit as if He had been hidden, making the Son even more felt and more efficient in His work. For the Trinity is "a monad taking its impetus from its superabundance, a dyad transcended (that is, it goes beyond the form and matter of which bodies consist), a triad defined by its perfection since it is the first to transcend the synthesis of duality in order that the Godhead might not be constricted or diffused without limit."[6] In the three Persons of the Godhead is plurality in unity, or perfect love, realized in both forms: expressed through relationships between Persons, but lived in complete unity. Everything in these three is in a direct relationship, for the Spirit is continually in the Father and the Son. If there were four, everything would not be in this direct, uninterrupted relationship. There would always be a "He" on the outside. It would be obvious that someone would always be left out. And in two Persons, once again would see something missing, a lack. In God three is everything.

The Spirit represents God's turning toward Himself, the regathering of His existence in personal communion. Without annulling this mode of being, deity is disclosed through the Spirit as structure, as an interpersonal center of infinite divinity, thus avoiding any lack of "generosity" of being that might be hermetically shut up in the darkness of an impersonal existence while also avoiding the disorder of infinite plurality. Both of these options would fill everything with an unfree, pantheistic essence, an essence without love and incapable of creation, subordinated to a blind, senseless law. Since the glorification of the Son, when humans could no longer see Him either in circumscribed space or in everything, the Son reveals Himself in the Spirit, who can be present everywhere. The Spirit radiates the resurrected body of Christ throughout all the world (cf. St. Basil, *On the Holy Spirit*).[7]

We shall see in another chapter how the Spirit puts each one of us in touch with Christ, but also how Christ is linked with the Spirit. This is the active practical form or the extension in us of what Christ did for us by cleansing us of passions, even through His own passion, and by glorifying us, through His resurrection, to the spiritualization of the body. This link between the work of Christ and of the Spirit appears even in the way in which the Spirit comes to subsistence, by proceeding from the Father to rest in the Son.

Chapter 8

The Spirit of Unity

Jesus Christ says that the Holy Spirit proceeds from the Father; He also says that He will send the Spirit to those who believe in Him (John 15:26). That is why in the Nicene-Constantinopolitan Creed the Church called the Spirit "[He] who proceeds from the Father." The Church Fathers wanted to emphasize that the proceeding of the Spirit from the Father is different from the begetting of the Son, but they did not wish to specify exactly what it involved. St. Gregory of Nazianzus says, "What, then, is 'proceeding'? You explain the ingeneracy of the Father and I will give you a biological account of the Son's begetting and the Spirit's proceeding—and let us go mad the pair of us for prying into God's secrets. . . . *In what particular, then,* it may be asked, *does the Spirit fall short of being Son? If there were not something missing, he would be Son.* We say there is no deficiency—God lacks nothing. It is their difference in, so to say, 'manifestation' or mutual relationship, which has caused the difference in names."[1]

St. Gregory illustrates the difference between the begetting of the Son by the Father and the proceeding of the Spirit by referring to the difference between Eve being made from Adam and Seth being born of Eve. He says, "People will say, *There cannot be two things, one an offspring and the other something else, coming from the single source.* Why not? Were not Eve and

Seth of the same Adam? Whose else? Were they both offspring? Certainly not. Yet they had a mutual identity—they were both human beings, nobody can gainsay that. You have grasped the possibility of our position by means of human illustrations, so will you stop fighting desperately against the Spirit for your view that he must either be an offspring or not consubstantial and not God?"[2]

All of the Church Fathers tried to emphasize that the Spirit, proceeding from the Father, rests in the Son. St. Gregory Palamas, basing himself on the testimony of John the Baptist, who said that he saw the Spirit descending from heaven and remaining on the Son (John 1:32–33), says that this is evidence that the Spirit rested upon the Son even before His incarnation. He shows St. John of Damascus thinking the same way. For, after he reminds us of the Gospel account in John 1:33, St. Gregory Palamas continues, "And so that some might not think that this was written and happened only with regards to the incarnation of the Son, let us listen to the divine Damascene, who wrote in the eighth chapter of his dogmatic writings, 'We believe also in the Holy Spirit . . . who proceeds from the Father and rests in the Son.'"[3]

This "resting" of the Spirit in the Son links the Spirit with the Son, a relationship that Catholicism mistakenly identified as the proceeding of the Spirit from the Father and from the Son as if from a single principle (*tanquam ex uno principio*). That formulation erases the distinction between the Father and the Son, considering the Spirit's proceeding as an action of their common essence and not one that maintains the Person of the Father distinct from that of the Son. St. Gregory Palamas considers the Spirit's "resting" in the Son as evidence of the Father's love for the Son. The Spirit is sent by the Father to rest in the Son as a demonstration of the Father's love for the Son. For the Father Himself is pleased to rest in the Son through the Spirit who proceeds from Him. But the Son does not remain passive and uncaring in the face of His Father's loving attention. He is pleased that the Father sends His Spirit to Him, and by accepting the Spirit He shows the Father His joy. St. Gregory Palamas says the following: "And the beloved Word and Son of God Himself turns towards the Begetter through the Holy Spirit, as love, and has the Holy Spirit from the Father, resting together with Him."[4]

To directly show someone your love for him gives him joy. But it is an even greater joy when another communicates and participates in that love. If the Father is the origin of the Son through the fact that in thinking of Himself He begets an image of Himself, only He can be the origin of the love that He has for the Son and that the Son has for Him; this is because, thinking of Himself as the loving Father of a Son, He comes to see Himself as another Person to whom He can show His love toward His image. In this relationship of love and joy that exists between the Father and Son from eternity, the Son cannot but remain a Son. In this sense, St. Gregory Palamas says, "That Spirit of the supreme Word is like an ineffable love of the Begetter towards the ineffably begotten Word himself. The beloved Word and Son of the Father also experiences this love towards the Begetter, but he does so inasmuch as he possesses this love as proceeding from the Father together with him and as resting connaturally in him. . . . [The Spirit] belongs also to the Son who possesses him from the Father as Spirit of truth, wisdom and word. For truth and wisdom constitute a word appropriate to the Begetter, a Word which rejoices together with the Father who rejoices in him."[5]

The Spirit does not proceed from the Father as an end in Himself, but the Spirit constitutes a loving tie formed between the Father and the Son. The Spirit is sent toward the Son as a Person who loves Him just as the Father does, so as to be a Person who loves the Son together with the Father. We see this when we say that the Spirit, proceeding from the Father, "rests in the Son, or shines forth from the Son."[6] Through this shining forth, the Spirit reveals the Father to the Son, and the Son to the Father. It is a reciprocity through which the Father never ceases to appear as Father nor the Son as Son.[7]

This does not mean that the Spirit is less of a Person than the Father or the Son. He is not simply an expression of the feelings of the Father and the Son. The Father shows the Son perfect love, rejoicing that there is another Person who proceeds from Him and who loves the Son together with Him. The Spirit receives this role from the Son as well. This role of loving together with the Father and the Son is shown in the fact that the Spirit is never named alone as "Lover," as the Father is called by the Son, or vice versa. We also see this in the fact that we say that we love the Spirit through the Father or through the Son, and we say that the Son or the Father gives us the Spirit, not the other way around.

But the Father does not beget the Spirit as another Son, for then He would not be sent toward the Son; rather, the Spirit has an independent position. The Father sends the Spirit to His only Son as evidence of His absolute love for the Son. The Spirit does not proceed from the Father just because the Son is begotten, and neither is the Son begotten in order that the Spirit might rest upon Him. This is why St. Gregory of Nazianzus says in *Oration 31* that the Son and the Holy Spirit are united not only by nature but also through the fact that the Son is born and the Spirit proceeds from the same Father. And the distinction between the Son and the Spirit is only that one is begotten and that the other proceeds. But it is good to remember first the begetting of the Son so that we can then say that the proceeding Spirit rests upon the begotten Son. But still the Spirit proceeds in order to rest upon the Son, and the Son is begotten of the Father who wants to have one on whom His Spirit can rest.

The Spirit is not a third Person either in the sense of being another Son or in the sense of being a "He" who is trapped in a closed relationship with the other two. The Spirit is in the Father, who loves the Son, as a Person who takes pleasure in the Son together with the Father and who comes from the Father to rest in the Son; He is in the Father as a Person who takes pleasure in the Father together with the Son, but as a Son in regard to the Father, and not as another Father. In that case He would not see the Father as a Father. The Spirit experiences the love between the Father and the Son, maintaining Their distinct characteristics of Father and Son. The Son loves the Spirit together with the Father. The Son is also present in this love, for He has the Spirit from His loving Father as the Father's Spirit. The Spirit proceeds from the

Father so as to increase the Father's joy in His Son, and the Son is begotten through the Father's desire to take joy in Him together with the Spirit. The fact that the Father uses the Spirit to convey His love deepens Their love and unity even more.

"You see how much I love You," the Father says to the Son, "having the Spirit who takes joy in You together with Me?" And the Son replies, "And You see how I respond in thanks by loving You together with the Spirit. I can love You as a Son only together with the Spirit whom You gave Me: never alone, but always with Him." The Father and the Son unite as Father and Son even more through the Spirit. They are three Persons, but the third does not stand to the side of the other two; He unites Them. He is in each, uniting Them and reinforcing Them in Their distinct qualities even when They speak with us. But this does not stop the Spirit from speaking to us Himself and from inspiring us to speak with the Father and the Son. He especially encourages us to pray to Them. Jesus told His disciples, "I still have many things to say to you, but you cannot bear them now. However, when He, the Spirit of truth, has come, He will guide you into all truth; for He will not speak on His own authority, but whatever He hears He will speak; and He will tell you things to come" (John 16:12–13). Both the Son and the Spirit speak with the other—and the Father—in Themselves. This is why we say that the Spirit is not a "He" about whom the Father and Son speak, but each speaks of the other two inseparably. Neither the Father nor the Son speaks about the Spirit as about a third who is apart from Them, but the Father has the Spirit within Himself when He speaks with the Son, and the Son has the Spirit within Himself when He speaks with the Father, just as when He speaks with us.

All three are continually united. The Father unites the Son and the Holy Spirit as the origin of both, of one through begetting and of the other as He proceeds toward the Son. The Son is united with the Father through the fact that He is begotten of the Father and has the Spirit who proceeds from the Father resting upon Him. The Spirit is united with the Father through the fact that He proceeds from Him, and with the Son through the fact that He rests upon Him. Each of the three divine Persons is united with the other two not only by Their common nature but also through Their personal qualities. The Spirit is called the Spirit of the Father and the Spirit of the Son: of the Father as the one from whom the Spirit proceeds toward the Son. But the Father is not called the Father of the Spirit, in the sense that He receives this characteristic through His relationship with the Spirit, and neither is the Son a Son of the Spirit, for He does not have His existence from the Spirit. Yet the Spirit is called both the Spirit of the Father and of the Son, His existence being bound to Them both. Just as the Son is the Father's, the Spirit is the Son's because He rests in Him. The Spirit is both the Father's and the Son's in the sense that the Trinity is completed in Their being. Each unites the other two, but the essence of the Trinity is completed only in the Spirit, and for this reason He is the one who brings the Father and the Son into Their ultimate union. Only through the Spirit does the Father show all of His love for the Son, and only through the Spirit does the Son show all of His love for the Father. Only through the Spirit does the Father activate all of His fatherly love for the Son, and likewise for the Son's filial love for the Father.

The proceeding of the Spirit from the Father toward the Son, as well as His shining forth from the Son toward the Father, is also reflected in the fact that we receive the Spirit from the Father through the Son and we can become loving sons of the Father in order to respond, together with the Son, to the Father's love. This establishes us in the love that exists between the Father and the Son, being beloved of the Father as His Son, loving the Father as our own and the Son as our Brother, which makes us love each other as sons of the same Father and as brothers of the same Son, who became our Brother when He took on human flesh. Perhaps this also partially shows us the role that "He" has in the relationship between "I" and "Thou." Each of us has Him in us, loving along with us, and this makes the love between us even greater.

But if the Son had not given us the Spirit to make us His own, and if the Son of the Father had not given us the Spirit of sonship, then we would not have that love which comes from being children of the Father and brothers of the Son. Holy Scripture often tells us that as the Son, Jesus Christ makes us children of the heavenly Father through the Spirit. The Apostle Paul says, "But when the fullness of the time had come, God sent forth His Son . . . to redeem those who were under the law, that we might receive the adoption as sons. And because you are sons, God has sent forth the Spirit of His Son into your hearts, crying out, 'Abba, Father!'" (Gal 4:4–6). So the Spirit eternally sustains in the Son the latter's love for His Father, as the one who proceeds from the Father for this very purpose. Therefore, when the Son became man, He had the Spirit of love from the Father so that He might communicate the Spirit to us as well. What Paul said above in Galatians he also says in his Epistle to the Romans: "For as many as are led by the Spirit of God, these are sons of God. . . . You received the Spirit of adoption by whom we cry out, 'Abba, Father'" (Rom 8:14–15). As such, we are also "heirs of God and joint heirs with Christ" (Rom 8:17). In this way, Christ became "the firstborn among many brethren" (Rom 8:29). As man, He bore His Spirit of divine sonship so as to share Him with us. In this way, the Holy Spirit is the one who unites us with God the Father and with the Son.

The Spirit unites with us so much that we experience as our own the emotion that He feels when He calls God "Father." But we still realize that if the Spirit had not united Himself with us, if He did not cry "Abba, Father" together with us, we could not cry out in this way by ourselves. This means that even before His incarnation, the Son's Spirit was not simply His own, but was also that of the Father, which is to say that the Son received the Spirit from the Father. It also means that the Spirit, through whom we cry "Abba, Father," is not separated from the Son. The incarnate Son cries out together with us, empowered by the same Spirit. But we do not only say "Abba, Father" through the Spirit. We also pray in the Spirit to the Father and the Son, and the Son prays together with the Spirit in us. We cannot pray to God the Father without the Spirit, and therefore neither without the Son. God, who desires to save us through the one whom He sent to us, gives us the power to seek His help: "Likewise the Spirit also helps in our weaknesses. For we do not know what we should pray for as we ought, but the Spirit Himself makes intercession for us with groanings which cannot be uttered" (Rom 8:26). Just as He unites the Son with the Father, so the Spirit unites us with the Father and the Son, so much that we cannot see the boundary between ourselves and God. Nonetheless, we still remain aware of our weaknesses. The Spirit does not remain simply a "He" for the Father and the Son, even when He is moving in us, but He becomes an "I" that is difficult to distinguish from our own, putting us in an "I-Thou" relationship with God.

St. Paul tells us that this beginning, of crying out and praying together with the Spirit of the Son, or with the Son dwelling in us through His Spirit, does not occur without a contribution on our part. But in this contribution we show that we strive to become like the Son as He was on earth, and the exalted and glorified Son desires that we travel the path that He trod in His body so that we too might arrive at the resurrection. Through His Spirit He draws us to become more and more like Him, even if we do not see it. He makes us children of the Father, resurrected, transfigured, and made holy, just like the incarnate and resurrected Son.

Chapter 9

SANCTIFICATION

The resurrected and glorified Son works in us through the Holy Spirit so that we too might travel the path toward sonship, upon which the body is transfigured or deified by the Spirit. The glorified Christ perfects this work in us through the Holy Spirit, just as He perfected it in His humanity while He was on earth. His Spirit guides us to the state to which the body of Christ was taken through resurrection, to the state of being transfigured with the body, super-illuminated, deified. This work of the glorified Son through the Spirit is a life-giving and sanctifying work. The Son could not complete this work in humans while He Himself was on earth, but only after His body was wholly penetrated by the life-giving and sanctifying Spirit. This life-giving and sanctifying work is that of the Son and the Spirit, or of the Son through the Spirit.

Thus the Spirit proceeds from the Father and rests in the Son not only to show the full extent of the loving unity between Father and Son—the love for the Son that comes from the Father and returns to the Father—but to bring to humans the love of the Son in whose image they were created, the love of the one who became a man in whom the Spirit could work so that the Spirit might pass through Him to all mankind. This work of the Spirit in the Son was first announced through the prophets, in order to turn them toward the Father, or to attract to the Father men who were united with the Son through faith and who were filled with the Spirit from the Son. This is why in the Nicene-Constantinopolitan Creed the Church called the Spirit not only "Holy" and the "Giver of life," but also the one "who spoke by the prophets." In this way, the preincarnate Word prepared men for the work that He was going to do, first while on earth, and later in men after He was glorified in His resurrected and deified body.

The common and complementary revelation of the Son and the Holy Spirit has a further development. Paul Evdokimov sees this development as an increasingly visible alternation of the works of the Spirit and of the Word—or, better said, of both. First one, then the other, reveals Himself in this common work. The Holy Spirit prepared the coming of the Word in a body. Christ first acted upon His body in a visible manner, but not without the presence of the Spirit working in Him, leading His body toward resurrection. They continued to work together after Christ rose again, and the Spirit's work, which had been invisible, was now tangibly manifest in the spiritualization of believers' bodies so as to resurrect them into the future life. "Through the mouths of the prophets, the entire Old Testament is a preliminary Pentecost in view of the advent of the Virgin and and of her *fiat* [cf. Luke 1:38]. . . . Pentecost appears as the ultimate purpose of the Trinitarian icon of salvation. Following the Church Fathers, it is even possible to say that Christ is the 'great Precursor of the Holy Spirit.'"[1] Evdokimov observes that the Holy Spirit and the Word are always together, but one comes to the forefront at certain times, and the other at other times. "During *Christ's earthly mission,* humanity's relation to the Holy Spirit occurred only through and in Christ. In contrast, *after Pentecost,* it is the relation to Christ that occurs only through and in the Holy Spirit. . . . The Ascension puts an end to the historical visibility of Christ. . . . But Pentecost gave the world back the interiorized presence of Christ and now reveals him not *before* but *inside* his disciples."[2]

The prophetic work of the Spirit of the preincarnate Word was necessary so that men might believe in Him when He miraculously came in a body. And it was necessary for the Son to come in a body so that God might truly adopt humanity in a body, leading it toward resurrection. But the work of the incarnate Son who was resurrected invisibly through the Holy Spirit was also necessary so that humans might lead an earthly life according to the model of Christ, in order to achieve a resurrected and spiritualized body like Christ's.

Western Christianity gives almost no weight to the Holy Spirit's work in men after Christ's ascension, nor to the ascended Christ's work through the Holy Spirit. Instead we see a break between Christ and the Holy Spirit. Christ is affirmed separately, as a Christ of discourse, not of uncreated grace dwelling in holy mystery, and not as the one who unites uncreated, sanctifying, transformative divine energy with our human subjectivities, raising believers to a new spiritual level. Only Orthodoxy speaks continuously about the life-giving and sanctifying work of the Holy Spirit, the one through whom Christ makes us children of God, with bodies that are resurrected and shine forth together with all of creation. For Orthodox Christians, humans are not forgiven only because of the superlative merit of Christ, or in order to be cleansed of sin only in the future life, through faith in the efficacy of His sacrifice. Rather, their lives grow in the imitation of Christ, in holiness, and their sanctification continues until it is realized in a transfigured body, in His likeness, in the future life through the Spirit of Christ. For Orthodoxy, God Himself bears humanity in a real sense, as the vehicle for transformation (transfiguration) and sanctification.

If we wish to achieve this goal, we too must exert ourselves so as to lead an earthly life that is as close as possible to the model of Christ. But even these efforts of ours to live as children of God are assisted by the Spirit of Christ. Our efforts begin in our rebirth through the Holy Spirit, who is given to us in Baptism. Then we leave the spiritual death of attachment to this world and cease to treat it as the only reality. The Spirit gives us birth into a true life in God and sustains us in it, and this is growth in holiness.

The Savior promises, on the one hand, that He will send the Spirit to those who believe in Him, and on the other hand, He says that they will receive Him for the first time in Baptism, so as to be born again and to become children of God, ceasing to be slaves of the material world (Gal 4:7–9). He says to Nicodemus, "Most assuredly, I say to you, unless one is born of water and the Spirit, he cannot enter the kingdom of God. That which is born of the flesh is flesh, and that which is born of the Spirit is spirit. . . . You must be born again" (John 3:5–7). But men are born as children of God because the incarnate Son of God unites with them through the Spirit. "As many as received Him [the Word], to them He gave the right to become children of God" (John 1:12). This is why the priest asks the one who has come to be baptized (or his godparent), "Do you renounce Satan?" and "Do you unite yourself with Christ?" And the latter responds in the affirmative to both questions. Christ comes through the Spirit, which is to say that through Christ comes the Spirit of the ascended Christ.

The work of the Holy Spirit is seen again in the request that the bread and wine be transformed into the body and blood of Christ: "We offer to You this spiritual worship without the shedding of blood, and we ask, pray, and entreat You: send down Your Holy Spirit upon us and upon these gifts here presented. And make this bread the precious Body of Your Christ. . . . And [make] that which is in this cup the precious Blood of Your Christ. . . . Changing them by Your Holy Spirit."[3] The entire Holy Trinity is at work here: the Father transforms the gifts, but through the Spirit, and the bread and wine cannot become the body and blood of Christ without Christ Himself wanting this to happen.

The forgiveness of sins also happens through the Holy Spirit. For Christ breathed and breathes the power of the Spirit over the apostles and their followers for the forgiveness of sins (John 20:22–23). The Son breathes the power of the forgiveness of sins over them, but this power is the Holy Spirit.

And the sanctifying of holy water, which in turn sanctifies everything that it touches, takes place through the Holy Spirit at the request of Christ. In the prayer for sanctifying the water, the priest addresses Him who came to bring healing to men: "And now send the grace of Your Holy and Life-Giving Spirit, who sanctifies all things, and sanctify this water." The Spirit is power breathed out by God, power that makes everything holy. The

Spirit proceeds ceaselessly from the Father and is sent through the Son to sanctify all things, to raise up the lives of men, and to heal all sickness when He so desires.

It is worth dwelling briefly on what it means to say that the Spirit is a life-giving and sanctifying Person, which is to say, to think about the way in which the work of the Spirit affects men. The Spirit is life-giving because He takes those who fell into transient pleasures and died, as well as those who continue to subsist in the poverty of egoism, and He delivers them from spiritual death, giving them a life that is ever higher and richer. That is why in the Trisagion Prayer the Father is called "God"; the Son "Mighty," as the one who overcame death by suffering it; and the Spirit "Immortal," because He gives us life when we are reborn through Baptism. This is a life of continuous spiritual growth, a life that is not weakened by spiritual death.

In his Epistle to the Romans, the Apostle Paul describes most profoundly the new life that the "Spirit of adoption" gives (Rom 8:15). He says that by becoming children of God through the Spirit, we also become heirs of the kingdom of heaven together with Christ. But this involves our glorification with Christ after suffering with Him: "If [we are] children, then . . . [we are] joint heirs with Christ, if indeed we suffer with Him, that we may also be glorified together. For I consider that the sufferings of this present time are not worthy to be compared with the glory which shall be revealed in us" (Rom 8:17–18).

We prepare for the glory of our future lives in God through suffering,[4] which we bear through the spirit of sonship that Christ gives us. But our suffering is meaningless unless we also have Christ, who strengthens us as we suffer the blows of evil and who helps us persevere during a life in which we submit, through faith, to all sorts of hardships and difficulties. That is why we receive Christ as a sacrifice in the Holy Eucharist: so that we too can bear a life of sacrifice, not yielding to pleasures. Christ lived this life of suffering as hunger, fatigue, mockery, blows, and crucifixion. Through His suffering His human nature was strengthened against the temptations of food, rest, worldly praises, and the fear of death. Through the power of the Spirit that He gives us,

He helps us to weaken and to overcome the passions of pleasure and egoism. It is a great mystery how Christ, although raised up as a man to a fully divine life, can give us the power to bear painful sufferings. He does not remain unfeeling in the face of our pain. It is somewhat analogous to the feelings of a mother who experiences her child's sufferings as if they were her own, helping the child to overcome them. The proclamation of His sufferings causes Jesus to relive them spiritually, together with the sufferings of those who experience them because of their love for Him. And deliverance from the passions of pleasure and egoism is the same as a life raised up, through relationship with God, to a realm that is no longer part of creation—into a more divine life, a life of holiness.

The goal of ascension in this life is the same as the effort of growing in the love of God, who unites us ever more closely with Himself. The Apostle Paul describes what it is like to have travelled this path: "I am persuaded that neither death nor life, nor angels nor principalities nor powers, nor things present nor things to come, nor height nor depth, nor any other created thing, shall be able to separate us from the love of God which is in Christ Jesus our Lord" (Rom 8:38–39). Through the Spirit we are "always carrying about in the body the dying of the Lord Jesus, that the life of Jesus also may be manifested in our body" (2 Cor 4:10). "For it is the God who commanded light to shine out of darkness, who has shone in our hearts to give the light of the knowledge of the glory of God in the face of Jesus Christ [as man]," who "is working for us a far more exceeding and eternal weight of glory" (2 Cor 4:6, 17). The divine Spirit is called "life-giving" and "holy" because He is the one in whom God the Father, through the Son, reaches us, bringing us all purity, praise, and divine sanctity.

The Spirit is called the divine breath, or a spiritual breeze that blows to us from the Father through the incarnate Son, a breeze that we sense from a realm above that of the world, as a breath of goodness, love, and purity. Through this breeze in us, the loving and completely holy Trinity is "like a wind," a spiritual "breath": a wind that you can hear but "cannot tell where it comes from and where it goes." So it is with anyone who is "born of the Spirit," as the Savior told Nicodemus (cf. John 3:5–8).

You experience the mystery of God in this mysterious breeze, yet He knows you too and makes you know yourself in God. And knowing God and knowing the way that leads to true realization, you no longer serve the transient world but God, who guarantees you eternal life. "But then, indeed, when you did not know God, you served those which by nature are not gods. But now after you have known God, or rather are known by God, how is it that you turn again to the weak and beggarly elements, to which you desire again to be in bondage?" (Gal 4:8–9).

No one can have faith in Christ, or knowledge of Christ's presence in himself, except through the Spirit. This shows how united the Spirit and Christ are in every believer. But along with belief in Christ and the pure and loving life of God, the Spirit also gives each person gifts that are appropriate to him. "No one can say that Jesus is Lord except by the Holy Spirit. There are diversities of gifts, but the same Spirit. . . . To one is given the word of wisdom through the Spirit, to another the word of knowledge through the same Spirit" (1 Cor 12:3–4, 8). And the different gifts of many people work together for the good of all. For the highest characteristic, toward which all travel through the Spirit, is love. Therefore, if someone has a great gift but has not love, he is a liar (cf. 1 Cor 13; 1 John 4:20). St. Basil the Great said that a person does not have his gifts for himself, but first and foremost so that he might use them for the good of others.

The importance that the Orthodox Church accords the Holy Trinity's work, through the Holy Spirit, in believers and in all of creation (a work that brings new and eternal life and holiness) is seen in the prayer to the Holy Spirit with which the Church begins some of its services. In this prayer we call the Holy Spirit "Heavenly King" because He raises us into the kingdom of heaven, where He rules as Spirit over material things. He is "Comforter" because He brings us comfort in the trials and difficulties of our earthly lives. He is "the Spirit of Truth" because He shows us the true way, which is life in Christ, the incarnate Son of God, or the Truth. He is "everywhere present," uniting everything in faith and love. He "fills all things," because He frees us from all want: He gives us life in God, who satisfies us completely. He is "Treasury of good things," for all good things come from Him, and through Him we can share them with others. In this way He completes everything. He is "Giver of life," freeing us from the poverty of lifeless existence, giving us eternal life. We ask Him to "come and abide in us" and to "cleanse us of every impurity," sanctifying us, and through this, to "save our souls."

Chapter 10

Praise to the Spirit of Life

In a book that was printed in Greek by the Patriarch of Constantinople in 1799 and then translated and published in Romanian at the Neamț Monastery in 1827, we find seven prayers to the Holy Spirit that are a true ascetic and mystical theology. They describe the spiritual path of purification in a nuanced, poetic manner that is rare these days. What they are talking about is the mystical state of union with God through the work of the Holy Spirit, who sustains the efforts of believers. The prayers are written by the leaders and spiritual servants of the Church, beginning with one by St. Symeon the New Theologian and continuing with others from the following centuries, as proof that throughout its history the Church has never ceased to express the experience of living in God through many different prayers. Professor Virgil Cândea brought this book to my attention, even acquiring a photocopy of it for me. I have transcribed the first prayer, which was written in Cyrillic characters, and added some commentary.

The first prayer shows the joy that the Holy Spirit brings to the soul and the unmixed unity that He works in the soul of the one who prays. It affirms the light that the Holy Spirit brings to the soul as He cleanses it of passions:

Come, true light. Come, eternal life. Come, hidden mystery. Come, nameless treasure. Come, ineffable reality. Come, inconceivable person. Come, endless bliss. Come, non-setting sun. Come, infallible expectation of all those who must be saved. Come, awakening of those who are asleep. Come, resurrection of the dead. Come, O Powerful One, who always creates and recreates and transforms by Your will alone. Come, O invisible and totally intangible and impalpable. Come, You who always remain motionless and at each moment move completely and come to us, asleep in hell, O, You, above all the heavens. Come, O beloved Name and repeated everywhere, but of whom it is absolutely forbidden for us to express the existence or know the nature. Come, eternal joy. Come, non-tarnishing crown. Come, purple of the great king our God. Come, crystalline cincture, studded with precious stones. Come, inaccesible sandal. Come, royal purple. Come, truly sovereign right hand. Come, You whom my miserable soul has desired and desires. Come, You the Lonely, to the lonely, since You see I am lonely. Come, You who have separated me from everything and made me solitary in this world. Come, You who have become Yourself desire in me, who have made me desire You, You, the absolutely inaccessible one. Come, my breath and my life. Come, consolation of my poor soul. Come, my joy, my glory, my endless delight.

I give You thanks that You have become one spirit with me, without confusion, without mutation, without transformation, You the God above everything, and that You have become all for me, inexpressible and perfectly gratuitous nourishment, which without end inexhaustibly flows to the lips of my soul and gushes out into the fountain of my heart, dazzling garment which destroys the devils, purification which bathes me with these imperishable and holy tears, that Your presence brings to those whom You visit. I give You thanks that for me You have become non-setting light, non-declining sun; for You who fill the universe with Your glory have nowhere to hide Yourself!

No, You have never hidden Yourself from anyone but we are the ones who always hide from You, by refusing to go to You; but then where could You hide, You who nowhere find the place of Your repose? Why would You hide, You who do not turn away from a single creature, who do not reject a single one? Today then, O Master, come pitch Your tent within me; until the end, make Your home and live continually, inseparably, within me, Your slave, O most kind One, that I also may find myself again in You, at my departure from this world and after my departure may I reign with You, God who is above everything.

O Master, stay and do not leave me alone, so that my enemies, arriving unexpectedly, they, who are always seeking to destroy my soul, may find You living within me and that they may take flight, in defeat, powerless against me, seeing You, You more powerful than everything, installed interiorly in the home of my poor soul. Yes, Master, just as You remembered me, when I was in the world and that in the midst of my ignorance, it is You who chose me and separated me from this world and set me before Your glorious face, so, now, keep me interiorly by Your dwelling within me, forever upright, resolute; that, by perpetually seeing You, I, the corpse, may live; that, by possessing You, I the begger, may always be rich, richer than kings that by eating and drinking You, by putting You on at each moment, I go from delight to delight in inexpressible blessings; for it is You who are all good and all glory and all delight and it is to You, holy, consubstantial and vivifying Trinity that the glory belongs, You whom all the faithful venerate, confess, adore and serve in the Father, the Son and the Holy Spirit, now and always and forever and ever. Amen.[1]

The second prayer to the Holy Spirit is "by John the Deacon, who was the brother of Mark, the Metropolitan of Ephesus, and jurist of the Churches in Constantinople." It seems that this refers to a brother of Metropolitan Mark of Ephesus, who in 1438 argued against the Catholic teaching on the *Filioque* clause at the Council of Florence. We first note in this prayer the expression "You who complete . . . the Trinity." For one Person would not be completely oriented toward the other, as Father and Son, except through love, or through the Spirit. The prayer also affirms that it is through the work of the Trinity that created things are perfected and deified. It says clearly that the entire Holy Trinity is seen in the completed work.

> Good Comforter, Holy Spirit, Spirit of Truth; You who proceed from the Father in ways that are hidden from men's understanding; You who complete the holy and life-giving Trinity, perfecting the oneness of our God; You who are worthy of praise together with the Father and the Son; You who are truly God and who truly deify men; You who sanctify and enlighten, dwelling in those who receive Your gift; You who build together with the original Mind and who work all things thought and felt together with the Word, together willing His coming among us and His taking on a body; You who sanctified our flesh in Him and who descended to the earth after His ascension into heaven; You who are in all places and who fill all things; You who showed Yourself as tongues of fire over the apostles and filled them with the gift of Your unspeakable power; You who through them led the whole world to a knowledge of the truth:
>
> Heavenly ruler, lover of men, lover of offerings, and giver of marvelous gifts, slow to anger and abounding in mercy, treasury of good things and giver of life—on this day and hour, and every time and place, when I cry out Your holy and glorified name from the depths of my unworthiness, look down from the heights of Your glory and search my affliction and my humility

with kindness. Do not be disgusted with me, O lover of goodness, because of my irreverent deeds, my evil thoughts, and my sins, from my youth until the present time. But as You guided Manasseh and David to repentance long ago, as the thief recognized You on the cross, as You turned the prostitute toward goodness, as You breathed the words of God into the prophets and spoke through them, as You help all those who are willing to walk in good deeds and in the fear of God even now and until the end of time, so too help me, a sinner, as I run to take hold of Your kindness and gifts.

Deliver me from the abyss of meaninglessness, from the depths of my blindness and ignorance, You who freed the world from the lies of the evil one. Sanctify me with Your life-giving power, for Yours is that holy light from which all goodness flowed into creation before the beginning of time. Burn up the immeasurable multitude of my errors, just as You consumed the cunning handiwork of the adversary in the immaterial fire of Your divinity. Crush his head beneath my feet and bring me peace. Fortify me with weapons of light. Defend me with the security of faith. Surround me with chains of righteousness. Consecrate my mouth with the Word of God. Righteous Spirit, renew that which is deep within me. Spirit of authority, strengthen my thoughts to keep them from slipping. Crown my thoughts with the eternal union of praise and virtue that can only come from You. Adorn me with good deeds, You who hold all of heaven's power in Your hands. Raise me up, good Comforter, according to the great bounty that You bestow upon men. Give me a spirit of wisdom, understanding, guidance, encouragement, knowledge, faithfulness, and the fear of God. Nourish me with Your holy fruits, You who fill all living things with goodwill and grace. Establish my life on dispassion and self-control. Enrich my heart with peaceful goodness. Buttress the dwelling place of my soul with the fortitude of faith.

Guard my thoughts with the tranquility of goodness. Correct my lethargy with long-suffering patience. Give sweet peace to the powers of my soul. Replace my sinful bitterness with overflowing joy, and complete my love for You with love for my neighbor.

Good Comforter, enlighten my mind with the brilliance of Your saving power, for it has been darkened by the fog of the passions. Make wise that part of it which has fallen prey to irreverence, and make it master of its desires. Lead it along the paths of Your righteous will. Warm my soul with Your life-giving gifts, for it has grown cold from lethargy and from sin's frosty touch. May my anger only strive against sin and the lying serpent. May my desire be only for You, the culmination of all longing. May my words be always controlled, and guide them according to Your holy will. May I bow before You in spirit and in truth, O God the Comforter, and may I serve You for all eternity. May I worship You, praise You, and thank You always, for You are forever glorified by the holy, bodiless powers.

Good Comforter, ever-righteous God, You are the fulfillment of all the mysteries of the Church. Through You I was born again, and through You I was rebuilt and renewed and drew near to God. Through You I was marked and sealed with royal unction, by God and by the giving of Your gift. Through You I was made worthy of the deathless table of the life-giving mysteries; I was made in the image of Christ, and [I was made a] god according to the gift. Yours is the efficacious priestly power that accompanies, keeps, and aids us. Yours are the innocence and purity that bring life to sinners who repent. Help me in the midst of my troubles. Sustain me with Your inexpressible power, Omnipotent One, and have mercy on my lethargy and indolence. Do not abandon me to the jibes of demons who destroy the soul. Do not leave me enslaved to shameful passions. You are quick to have mercy, so grant that I might live

> out my days in purity and in the fear of God, until such a time when this life ends and eternal life has ripened. Then my joy will be complete, for I will be truly pure and will have proof of all Your heavenly goodness. Then will I praise You, O God the Comforter. Then will I worship, thank, and bow before You, together with the Father and Son, forever and ever. Amen.[2]

Note in particular that in this prayer the mystery of anointing with holy oil is considered an act of anointing the believer as a king in the kingdom of heaven, and the Holy Spirit Himself is the one who effects all mysteries and all sanctifying acts through the priest. Also note the expressions "the abyss of meaninglessness," and "the depths of . . . ignorance," out of which the Spirit rescues us. The abyss of meaninglessness is the opposite of the abyss of life in God, and the depths of ignorance are the opposite of the infinite knowledge in which it is possible to progress in God. One can oppose infinite life with meaninglessness, and knowledge with its limitation, for God does not completely unmake conscious created beings, but He does allow them to move ever further away from His infinite positive. The power of sanctification, it says in the prayer, is always purifying. The more you grow in life, the purer you are, and vice versa. For life, being one with God, is one with goodness and generosity. Finally, note the expression "peaceful goodness." Goodness fears nothing. It is generous because it feeds on infinite life.

The third prayer to the Holy Spirit presents the Holy Spirit more precisely as the one who leads the believer on the ascetic path toward mystical union with God.

> Good Spirit, Holy Giver of Life, I fall before You guilty of all of my deeds and worthy of punishment. To You I pray, my Lord and my God, Life eternal and unfading, true and uncreated Light. Do not annihilate me completely, but establish Yourself in me as Lord. For Your power is omnipotent and untold: full, uncircumscribed, and intangible Lordship. You are entirely good and are the cause of all good and useful things. You

renew and build up all flesh, giving strength to the weak. We are born again in You, created a second time. In You is all knowledge, which illuminates our minds so that we might see the Lord, our Savior. In Him is life, wisdom beyond words, knowledge that surpasses the senses, brightness beyond understanding—all life, all power, all glory—for He is the God who carries our burdens and forgives us. Make me entirely Yours. Give me life according to Your will. Resurrect those parts of me that sin has brought down. Enlighten my heart, which is darkened by evil desires, and bring life to my soul, which is dead in its sin. Unfurl the threefold mantle of my passions. Have mercy on me in my poverty. Deliver me from every enemy who, from without or within, rises up over me. Deliver me from every evil thing. Forgive my reprehensible deeds, and plant Your perfect love inside of me.

Write Your servant's name in the Book of Life, and give me a good end so that, as I rise victorious over the devil, I might bow confidently before Your kingly throne. Make my heart good soil, Lord, and sow it with good seeds. Cover me with Your grace like the morning dew, and harvest that which is good: humble prayer, restraint, watchfulness, and tears. Return my soul to rest, through fasting. Return my soul to heaven's shelter through heavy sufferings and adversity. May my soul, O Lord, find itself, together with all the saints, within Your indescribable light. Hear me, Lord of all, uncircumscribed and beyond understanding, although I am merely Your miserable and unworthy servant. Help me to walk the straight and narrow path to its end so that I might prove Your promises true and shout aloud in the midst of heaven's delights: Praise be to the immortal Father, the immortal Son, and the immortal Spirit, adoration and worship forever and ever. Amen.[3]

This prayer describes the way of ascetic trials as a narrow path, closed to the pleasurable passions and winding through the unpleasant ones: overcoming difficulties and hardships with faith in the will of God, and thus arriving at illumination through the Holy Spirit and an ever-deeper sanctification, which will be obtained completely in the future life. These gifts grow in the heart when it becomes good soil, fruitful and accepting of the Holy Spirit's seeds. Fasting is the power that gives rest to the soul, which is freed from the worries of pleasant food. In this state of rest, the soul can focus on God alone, and the abundant gifts of the Holy Spirit can enter its heart.

The fourth prayer to the Holy Spirit:

> Come, ever-truthful, ever-faithful Spirit, Creator of the world. Come and search our hearts with Your unsurpassable wisdom. Come in Your omnipotence and Your immutability, You who are beyond description and understanding. Come in Your unlimited power, grace, and goodness, You who have no equal. Come, You who crown creation with glory and are so great that nothing in it can contain You. Come, You who are both life and the spring of life, both power and the origins of power, both wisdom and He from whom all wisdom flows. Come, You who are slow to anger and abounding in love, the true wisdom of all those who want to be saved. Come, You who are alone, to the alone, for I am alone, as You see me here. Come and dwell in me, purifying me of all incursions and infestations of the adversary.
>
> We worship You, good and mighty King, for in You we breathe, think, and know God. We worship You, for You show us the beauty of the heavens: the path of the sun, the orb of the moon, the starry array, moving together in sublime unison. We worship You, for You teach us to understand the times: the changing seasons, the regenerating winds, the circular motion of the years. We thank You, for from You we have the promise of the kingdom of heaven: the chorus of

angels and the multitudes at worship. We see it now through mirrors and prophecies, but after a short time we shall know it fully. We thank You, for You give us new skill at earthly works: food, crafts, laws, habits, good deeds, and good behavior.

What tongue can express Your greatness, O Lord? You are the pure and holy spring that never dries up. You are the unfathomable depths of wisdom and power. You are life and immortality, which is boundless and immeasurable. You are knowledge and a wealth of understanding that is never emptied or lessened. You are goodness and a treasury of mercy for all the world, never emptied or spent. You breathed into the prophets and told them of things to come. You proclaimed the incarnation of the only begotten Son before it took place. You came to Mary with grace, to her who was chosen from among the peoples before the beginning of time, as one innocent and without sin. You made her womb into a holy dwelling place for God the Word and, together with the Father, You brought Him into the world. Being one with Christ in essence, together You worked divine wonders while He was on earth. And once He had ascended into heaven and was seated as God at the right hand of the Father, You descended upon the apostles in tongues of fire, filling them with words, wisdom, daring, and power.

Thus I pray to You, I fall before You: turn Your eyes upon me and overcome me, Your servant. Search me with Your goodness and deliver me from the miserable abyss of my errors, whether deliberate or unknown. Cleanse both my body and my soul of filth. Sanctify me; give me wisdom and understanding. Guide me toward saving knowledge, and make me strong against temptation, stronger than all adversaries that come against me. Breathe into me gentleness, long-suffering, truth, righteousness, silence, and the foundation of all good works: self-control. Make me a church worthy to wor-

> ship You. Be my Lord, my Shepherd, and my Benefactor. For You are the fulfillment of all good things. I give praise to You, together with the Father and the Son, today, tomorrow, and forevermore. Amen.[4]

This is a prayer that asks for the Holy Spirit to come with great pleading. It praises the way He works together with the Father to create and sustain the world in its wonderful order; it also praises His foreknowledge: that He would contribute to the miraculous incarnation of the Son and would work in the incarnate Son, together with the Father, and also in the glorification of Christ. It reiterates that He breathes into us not only new natural life but also that life that is higher than nature and that helps all things grow. For this reason, the prayer affirms that He makes faithful men into the Church, full of the Spirit's praise now and even more completely in the life to come.

The entire dialogue between God and human beings takes place through the Holy Spirit. Through the Holy Spirit, God sends human beings His love for them, and they receive this love and nurture it through the love with which they respond to the divine love. This effects the eternal deification of man in the kingdom of heaven.

NOTES

Chapter 1

1. Gregory of Nazianzus, *Oration 31: On the Holy Spirit*, in *On God and Christ: The Five Theological Orations and Two Letters to Cledonius*, trans. Frederick Williams and Lionel Wickham (Crestwood, NY: St. Vladimir's Seminary Press, 2002), 134.

2. Maximus the Confessor, *Questions to Thalassius* 13 (Patrologia Graeca [PG] 90:296), in *Filocalia*, trans. Dumitru Stăniloae, 2nd ed. (Bucharest: Humanitas, 1999), 3:63.

3. Maximus the Confessor, *Questions to Thalassius* 19 (PG 90:308), in Stăniloae, *Filocalia*, 3:74 [the bracketed words in this quotation are Fr. Stăniloae's – trans.].

4. Gregory of Nazianzus, *Oration 28: On the Doctrine of God*, in *On God and Christ*, 38–39.

5. Ibid., 39.

6. Ibid.

7. Ibid., 40.

Chapter 2

1. All biblical quotations are taken from *The Orthodox Study Bible* (Nashville, TN: Thomas Nelson, 2008).

Chapter 3

1. Athanasius, *Against the Arians (Orationes Contra Arianos IV)*, Oration 3.66 (Nicene and Post-Nicene Fathers, Series 2 [NPNF^2] 4:430). [The Romanian edition incorrectly gives this reference as Athanasius, *Contra Arianos*, Oration 1, PG 26:48. - trans.]

2. Gregory of Nyssa, *Against Eunomius* 8.5 (NPNF^2 5:207). Cf. Basil of Caesarea, *Contra Eunomium* 2.12 (PG 29:593A–B).

3. Gregory of Nazianzus, *Oration 31*, in *On God and Christ*, 128.

4. Ibid., 127–128.

5. John of Damascus, *Exposition of the Orthodox Faith* 1.8 (NPNF^2 9:513).

6. "The Office for the Burial of a Layman," in *The Great Book of Needs*, vol. 3, *The Occasional Services* (South Canaan, PA: St. Tikhon's Seminary Press, 2002), 189.

7. Basil the Great, *Letter 38* (NPNF^2 8:139).

8. Ibid.

9. Ibid.

10. Athanasius, *De Synodis* (NPNF^2 4:464). [Although Stăniloae attributes this phrase to Athanasius, Athanasius was quoting from the heretical "Macrostich" written by Eusebian bishops in 344 CE. - trans.]

11. Gregory of Nazianzus, *Oration 31*, in *On God and Christ*, 127–128.

12. Ibid., 128.

13. Ibid.

Chapter 4

1. "Preparatory Prayers for Holy Communion," in *Prayer Book* (Jordanville, NY: Holy Trinity Monastery, 1960), 326.

2. Gregory of Nazianzus, *Oration 29: On the Son*, in *On God and Christ*, 70–71.

3. Maximus the Confessor, *Questions to Thalassius* 25 (PG 90:332), in Stăniloae, *Filocalia*, 3:97–98.

4. Maximus the Confessor, *Questions to Thalassius* 25, Scholion 6 (PG 90:337), in Stăniloae, *Filocalia*, 3:101.

5. Maximus the Confessor, *Questions to Thalassius* 25, Scholion 10 (PG 90:337), in Stăniloae, *Filocalia*, 3:102.

6. Maximus the Confessor, *Questions to Thalassius* 25, Scholion 12 (PG 90:337–339), in Stăniloae, *Filocalia*, 3:102.

7. Basil the Great, *Homily 16: On the Text "In the Beginning Was the Word"* (PG 31:477–479), in *Scrieri*, pt. 1, trans. Dumitru Fecioru, Părinți și Scriitori Bisericești 17 (Bucharest: Editura Institutului Biblic și de Misiune al Bisericii Ortodoxe Române, 1986), 517–518.

Chapter 5

1. Maximus the Confessor, *Letter 2: On Love; To John the Cubicularius,* in Andrew Louth, ed. and trans., *Maximus the Confessor* (London and New York: Routledge, 1996), 84.

2. Ibid., 85.

3. Ibid.

4. Ibid., 86.

5. Gregory of Nazianzus, *Oration 29,* in *On God and Christ,* 86–87.

Chapter 7

1. Athanasius of Alexandria, *Lettres à Sérapion sur la Divinité du Saint-Esprit,* trans. Joseph Lebon, Sources chrétiennes 15 (Paris: Éditions du Cerf, 1947), 129.

2. Gregory Palamas, *The One Hundred and Fifty Chapters,* chap. 36, ed. and trans. Robert E. Sinkewicz (Toronto: Pontifical Institute of Mediaeval Studies, 1988), 123.

3. Pavel Florensky, *The Pillar and Ground of the Truth: An Essay in Orthodox Theodicy in Twelve Letters,* trans. Boris Jakim (Princeton, NJ: Princeton University Press, 1997), 37–38.

4. Gregory of Nazianzus, *On the Holy Spirit,* in *On God and Man: The Theological Poetry of St. Gregory of Nazianzus,* trans. Peter Gilbert (Crestwood, NY: St. Vladimir's Seminary Press, 2001), 45.

5. Basil of Caesarea, *Contra Eunomium,* bk. 4 (PG 29:756).

6. Gregory of Nazianzus, *Oration 23,* in *St. Gregory of Nazianzus: Select Orations,* trans. Martha Vinson, The Fathers of the Church 107 (Washington, DC: The Catholic University of America Press, 2003), 137.

7. Basil the Great, *On the Holy Spirit,* trans. David Anderson (Crestwood, NY: St. Vladimir's Seminary Press, 1980).

Chapter 8

1. Gregory of Nazianzus, *Oration 31,* in *On God and Christ,* 122–123.

2. Ibid., 125.

3. Gregory Palamas, *Address 1,* in Joseph Bryennios, *Cuvinte douăzeci și două pentru purcederea prea Sfântului Duh* (Buzău, Romania, 1832), 80–81. [The reference is to John of Damascus, *Exposition of the Orthodox Faith* 1.8. – trans.]

4. Quoted in Archimandrite Kiprian Kern, *Antropologiâ Sv. Grigoriâ Palamy* [in Russian] (Paris: YMCA Press, 1950), 356.

5. Gregory Palamas, *One Hundred and Fifty Chapters,* chap. 36, p. 123.

6. Gregory of Cyprus (PG 142:240, 242, 257, 260, 267, 286).
7. Bryennios, *Cuvinte douăzeci și două*, 80–81.

Chapter 9

1. Paul Evdokimov, *L'Esprit Saint dans la tradition orthodoxe* (Paris: Éditions du Cerf, 1969), 87, 89.
2. Ibid., 90.
3. *The Divine Liturgy of Saint John Chrysostom: A New Translation by Members of the Faculty of Hellenic College/Holy Cross Greek Orthodox School of Theology*, 4th ed. (Brookline, MA: Holy Cross Orthodox Press, 2009), 22.
4. [The Romanian word "*patimă*" refers both to the passions (i.e., to what Clement of Alexandria calls "an excessive feeling, or appetite, going beyond what is reasonable") and to physical suffering, particularly to the sufferings (the "passion") of Christ. Stăniloae uses the word in both senses in this paragraph, and it has been rendered into English as either "suffering" or "passion" depending on the context, but the reader should keep in mind the close relationship between the two in Orthodox theology. – trans.]

Chapter 10

1. Symeon the New Theologian, *Invocation to the Holy Spirit*, in *Hymns of Divine Love*, trans. George A. Maloney (Denville, NJ: Dimension Books, n.d.), 9–10.
2. *Rugăciunile sfinților părinți (Apanthisma)*, trans. Neamț Monastery (Bucharest: Cartea Ortodoxă, 2007), 180–184.
3. Ibid., 200–201.
4. Ibid., 216–218.

Bibliography

Athanasius of Alexandria. *Lettres à Sérapion sur la Divinité du Saint-Esprit*. Translated by Joseph Lebon. Sources chrétiennes 15. Paris: Éditions du Cerf, 1947.

Basil the Great. *Scrieri,* pt. 1. Translated by Dumitru Fecioru. Părinţi şi Scriitori Bisericeşti 17. Bucharest: Editura Institutului Biblic şi de Misiune al Bisericii Ortodoxe Române, 1986.

Bryennios, Joseph. *Cuvinte douăzeci şi două pentru purcederea prea Sfântului Duh*. Buzău, Romania, 1832.

The Divine Liturgy of Saint John Chrysostom: A New Translation by Members of the Faculty of Hellenic College/Holy Cross Greek Orthodox School of Theology. 4th ed. Brookline, MA: Holy Cross Orthodox Press, 2009.

Evdokimov, Paul. *L'Esprit Saint dans la tradition orthodoxe*. Paris: Éditions du Cerf, 1969.

Florensky, Pavel. *The Pillar and Ground of the Truth: An Essay in Orthodox Theodicy in Twelve Letters*. Translated by Boris Jakim. Princeton, NJ: Princeton University Press, 1997.

The Great Book of Needs. Vol. 3, *The Occasional Services*. South Canaan, PA: St. Tikhon's Seminary Press, 2002.

Gregory of Nazianzus. *On God and Christ: The Five Theological Orations and Two Letters to Cledonius*. Translated by Frederick Williams and Lionel Wickham. Crestwood, NY: St. Vladimir's Seminary Press, 2002.

______. *On God and Man: The Theological Poetry of St. Gregory of Nazianzus*. Translated by Peter Gilbert. Crestwood, NY: St. Vladimir's Seminary Press, 2001.

———. *St. Gregory of Nazianzus: Select Orations*. Translated by Martha Vinson. The Fathers of the Church 107. Washington, DC: The Catholic University of America Press, 2003.

Kern, Kiprian. *Antropologiâ Sv. Grigoriâ Palamy* [in Russian]. Paris: YMCA Press, 1950.

Louth, Andrew, ed. and trans. *Maximus the Confessor*. London and New York: Routledge, 1996.

The Nicene and Post-Nicene Fathers. Series 2. Edited by Philip Schaff and Henry Wace. 14 vols. Oxford and New York, 1890–1900.

The Orthodox Study Bible. Nashville, TN: Thomas Nelson, 2008.

Palamas, Gregory. *The One Hundred and Fifty Chapters*. Edited and translated by Robert E. Sinkewicz. Toronto: Pontifical Institute of Mediaeval Studies, 1988.

Patrologia graeca. Edited by Jacques-Paul Migne. 161 vols. Paris, 1857–1886.

Prayer Book. Jordanville, NY: Holy Trinity Monastery, 1960.

Rugăciunile sfinților părinți (Apanthisma). Translated by Neamț Monastery. Bucharest: Cartea Ortodoxă, 2007.

Stăniloae, Dumitru, trans. *Filocalia*. 2nd ed. Bucharest: Humanitas, 1999.

Symeon the New Theologian. *Hymns of Divine Love*. Translated by George A. Maloney. Denville, NJ: Dimension Books, n.d.

CPSIA information can be obtained at www.ICGtesting.com
Printed in the USA
BVOW08s0556110316

439803BV00001B/2/P